the woman of mystery

the woman of mystery

Unveiling the Secret to True Romance

Hayley DiMarco

TYNDALE HOUSE PUBLISHERS, INC.
Carol Stream, Illinois

Hungry Planet

Visit Tyndale's exciting Web site at www.tyndale.com

Visit Hungry Planet's mysterious Web site at www.hungryplanetmedia.com

TYNDALE and Tyndale's quill logo are registered trademarks of Tyndale House Publishers, Inc.

The Woman of Mystery: Unveiling the Secret to True Romance

Copyright © 2009 by Hungry Planet. All rights reserved.

Cover photo of woman copyright © by Tracy Kahn/Corbis. All rights reserved.

Interior photograph on page 2 copyright © by Barbara Henry/iStockphoto. Interior photographs on pages 18, 98, 148, and 164 copyright © by Photos.com. Interior photographs on pages 54 and 118 copyright © by Shutterstock. Interior photograph on page 80 copyright © by Fanelie Rosier/iStockphoto. Interior photograph on page 132 copyright © by David Mehary/iStockphoto. All rights reserved.

Cover concept and design direction by Hungry Planet

Interior design by Jennifer Ghionzoli

Edited by Stephanie Voiland

Published in association with the literary agency of Yates & Yates, LLP, 1100 Town & Country Road, Suite 1300, Orange, CA 92868.

Unless otherwise indicated, all Scripture quotations are taken from the *Holy Bible*, New Living Translation, copyright © 1996, 2004, 2007 by Tyndale House Foundation. Used by permission of Tyndale House Publishers, Inc., Carol Stream, Illinois 60188. All rights reserved.

Scripture quotations marked ESV are from *The Holy Bible*, English Standard Version®, copyright © 2001 by Crossway Bibles, a publishing ministry of Good News Publishers. Used by permission. All rights reserved.

Scripture quotations marked KJV are taken from *The Holy Bible*, King James Version.

Scripture quotations marked *The Message* are taken from *The Message* by Eugene H. Peterson, copyright © 1993, 1994, 1995, 1996, 2000, 2001, 2002. Used by permission of NavPress Publishing Group. All rights reserved.

Scripture quotations marked NIV are taken from the HOLY BIBLE, NEW INTERNATIONAL VERSION®. NIV®. Copyright © 1973, 1978, 1984 by International Bible Society. Used by permission of Zondervan. All rights reserved.

Library of Congress Cataloging-in-Publication Data

DiMarco, Hayley.
   The woman of mystery : unveiling the secret to true romance / Hayley DiMarco.
      p. cm.
   Includes bibliographical references and index.
   ISBN 978-1-4143-2468-5 (sc : alk. paper) 1. Women—Religious aspects—Christianity.
2. Christian women—Religious life. 3. Man-woman relationships—Religious aspects—
Christianity. I. Title.
   BT704.D55 2009
   261.8'35—dc22   2008045452

Printed in the United States of America

15 14 13 12 11 10 09
 7   6   5   4   3

TO MY HUSBAND,
thank you for loving me even when I fail to keep the mystery alive.

AND TO MY DAUGHTER,
that I might teach you the art of mystery for a life of true romance.

We need a witness to our lives. There's a billion people on
the planet. . . . I mean, what does any one life mean? But in a
marriage, you're promising to care about everything. The good
things, the bad things, the terrible things, the mundane things
. . . all of it, all the time, every day. You're saying, "Your life will
not go unnoticed because I will notice it. Your life will not go
unwitnessed because I will be your witness."
• SHALL WE DANCE

Sometimes the only way to catch an uncatchable woman is to
offer her a wedding ring.
• BIG FISH

Have you ever felt remarkable? Was there a time in your
life when you remember feeling lovely, attractive, and
alluring? Or have you wondered if feeling that way is even
possible? And what about mystery? Do you feel like a mystery waiting to be unraveled by the man in your life? Or
do you feel more like a practical, hardworking woman
who is too often taken for granted? Or maybe more like an
undiscovered diamond in the rough, waiting for the right
man to find you? As women, we all crave the magic—that
delightful tingle that runs over our skin, that sense of feeling like a princess, that excitement that accompanies the

unknown, that elation that comes from being truly known and loved. But for most of us, life isn't a fairy tale; it comes at us fast and leaves little time for mystery and intrigue.

Does it have to be that way? Or is there something at work just under the surface of our day-to-day reality that hasn't been discovered yet? In the midst of our everyday lives of commuting to work, doing the laundry, and living out relationships with other flawed human beings, is there really a place for romance and mystery?

I was single until I was thirty-seven years old. And believe me, it felt like an eternity. Sure, I had some moments of great romance, times when I was sure this must be the one, and then he'd disappoint me or just leave. Romance was a roller coaster that I both hoped to ride and feared to fall off of. And it was an ever-present thought at the very center of my heart.

When I was *finally* dating my husband, Michael, it was amazing. I felt more beautiful than I had ever felt before. I felt like I was a prize, highly valued and sought after. I looked different to myself when I looked in the mirror, and I certainly felt different inside. The mystery was alive for both of us, and it's what kept us chasing after more time with each other.

But is it realistic to think this kind of mystery and romance can be part of our daily lives, no matter what life stage we're in? For the single woman, is it possible to continue to believe that true romance is possible, even after getting your heart broken time after time and finding yourself home alone on yet another Saturday night? And for the woman who is married, is it possible to keep the romance alive as you look around at the dirty dishes, the piles of laundry, and the whining child and feel more utilitarian than mysterious?

At its most fundamental level, mystery is eternal. It is the evidence of an eternal God in the life of an eternal soul. And when a woman finds mystery within her, she finds herself miraculously and mysteriously in possession of everything she needs, even when the circumstances around her say otherwise. The mystery this book speaks of is the mystery of hope, peace, and love fully fusing with daily life. It is the mystery of a woman so secure in who she is that nothing—no circumstance or danger or setback—can shake her. It is the mystery found in the woman who can say, "It is well with my soul," and though the waves should crash and the sea billows roll, she will not crumble. Mystery is that essential element of character in the woman who rests in the knowledge that God is all she needs, and because of that, nothing she lacks can distract her. She knows the power her words have on the lives of those around her. She doesn't let the world dictate how she presents herself. She makes her home a refuge. Her heart is open to both receiving love and giving it. And she knows that the truest romance of all is found in the love that Christ the Bridegroom has for his bride.

I have to be honest; I feel completely incapable of writing a book on mystery. I mean, I understand the concept. I've studied it, I've practiced it, I've taught it to others, and I love it. But the truth is, more days than not, I don't feel it. There are many days when I am short with my husband, when I am frustrated with my life, and when I wonder what ever happened to the moments of mystery I've experienced. I worry, I fear, and I yell. But I think that maybe that is exactly what qualifies me to write this book. I understand how it feels to be deflated and lonely. I know how emotions can whisper little lies about life and get me all jumbled up inside. I know the pull of a driven life. I know the joy of success and the excitement of calling my own shots, and yet I can say with confidence that none of it compares to living in the mystery. I have discovered that mystery is tied to something far greater than me. And I have found mystery to be more alluring and exciting than anything this earth has to offer. I know this all sounds rather abstract right now, but bear with me. Mystery is an elusive thing, not easily touched, let alone captured. It takes time and effort, but it is worth every moment. Mystery will lift you above the fray and show you a view of your world you may never have seen before.

So let's lift the veil of the Woman of Mystery and see how she does it.

woman an adult female person

mystery whatever resists or defies explanation

the Woman of Mystery

I would rather have had one breath of her hair, one kiss from her mouth, one touch of her hand, than eternity without it. One.
• CITY OF ANGELS

I'd rather fight with you than make love to anyone else.
• THE WEDDING DATE

You're a woman and you want him to appreciate you because of that. Being female is at the core of who you are, and you want him to notice. To notice your ability to communicate and the funny way you wiggle your nose when you're happy. You hope he will catch the curve of your legs and the way you fixed your hair. You want him to follow the scent that lingers as you walk by. You want to allure the man you desire, and you realize that it takes all that is feminine in you to do it. But you also want him to love the parts of your personality that make you uniquely you: Your self-assertiveness and your ability to have strong opinions and ideas. Your sense of humor, your favorite and unfavorite things, the quirky habits that set you apart from everyone else. Your shyness, your strength. You want him to recognize your mind and all its creativity and power, your heart and its ability to love, your soul and its depth. You want him to find in you that thing he's been looking for all his life.

Romance arrives when you realize that on all these counts he has seen you and found you alluring. In return, he shows honor and respect for those things in you that he finds so appealing. When he showers praise on your very essence, you are where you long to be—in the heart of romance. All that we define as romantic has the element of recognition in it. We are recognized for who we are, and we are loved for who we are. We are recognized as "other," as different from the one who sees us, but still awe-inspiring. When a man finds everything about you (even your idiosyncrasies) endearing, he is offering you pure romance. And it is intoxicating.

If you are like me, there is likely a part of you that is craving romance. Maybe you've tried to stuff it into the corner of your heart, or maybe you've tried to ignore it altogether. But it's there, whether you acknowledge it or not. Like me, you might have tried to fulfill your need for romance with fantasies of romantic moments with a man, sexy clothes, romantic getaways, or idyllic decor . . . and more than likely, you've come up short. The romance your mind promises your heart never seems to arrive. And so you yearn for more, and you wonder what you are doing wrong—or what's wrong with you. The search for romance seems never ending and always just out of reach.

But it doesn't have to be this way. When we embrace the concept of womanhood as God designed it to be, true romance is possible. At her best, the Woman of Mystery is an echo of the divine, revealed in the romance of femininity (more on this in a moment). Her presence can transform a room. She is captivating and inviting, and men find her unforgettable. If romance is a kind of aphrodisiac for women, then one could say that mystery is an aphrodisiac for men. The mystery of the woman who can't be fully understood is an invitation to the masculine heart to come closer.

This woman is alluring and warm. She draws people to her. People who know her want what she has; people who observe her are intrigued by her charm and charmed by her beauty, though that beauty might be just beneath the surface. It is the atmosphere that surrounds her that entices others to her side. It is her soul that makes people curious, that causes them to follow her, pursue her, and want to know her.

Though mystery can keep many a man guessing, it is also what makes him desire a woman. Mystery says to the man who catches a glimpse of it, "That is something special," and it compels him to explore the depths of it. But more than that, it can give him strength and hope. Mystery leaves his soul wanting more, so when a woman allows some things to remain hidden or unspoken, he is intrigued.

There are some women throughout history who have given us a peek at the mystery that captivates. Jackie Kennedy was one such woman who lived with a captivating sense of grace and dignity. She will forever be remembered as a woman who didn't allow her grief and pain to become the focal point of her life. She maintained her personal strength in order to be strong for her nation. Lady Diana also had an air of mystery that endeared her to the world. Even in the midst of her own heartache, she reached out to the world and sought to bring comfort to the weak and neglected. Audrey Hepburn kept a certain sense of mystery about her throughout her life too, not only because of her physical beauty and the way she carried herself, but also because of her dedication to helping underprivileged children in the poorest countries. She will live on in the minds of generations as a result. These women didn't just let it all hang out; they lived with gentle reserve and unspoken confidence. They weren't prone to fits of rage or given to public displays of emotional weakness or excess. Though their mystery might not have come from a life lived with Christ, they are still noteworthy starting points of what mystery looks like.

Feminine figures in the faith like Kay Arthur and Beth Moore demonstrate a compelling sense of mystery in their own way. They speak to thousands with confidence and yet also speak to individual women they meet with such charm that each woman believes, at that moment, that she is the only person in the world. I have personally watched Kay interact with hundreds of women and have seen how she treats each stranger as a friend. She looks into these women's eyes as they share their hearts with her. She holds their hands and hugs them tight. Her mind isn't on herself or her next appointment but always on those she is with. This kind of compassion and love captivates anyone in her presence. It gives her an air of kindness and strength that draws people to her. God's love is quickly seen in the lives of women like these.

The Mysterious Christ

"I want them to have complete confidence that they understand God's mysterious plan, which is Christ himself. In him lie hidden all the treasures of wisdom and knowledge" (Colossians 2:2-3).

Christ himself is the author of mystery. His very presence here on earth was a mystery (see 1 Timothy 3:16). He maintained that mystery as he spoke in parables, suggesting that not all who listened would understand (see Luke 8:9-10). And in a way that defies human logic, when he was being persecuted, he didn't seek to defend himself or argue with his persecutors but instead accepted their attacks with a sense of acceptance that God's hand was in the matter (see 1 Peter 2:23).

Imagine how he walked while he lived among us; imagine how he talked and loved while he interacted with people. Imagine the calm he instilled in them. Imagine how captivating his words would have been to hungry hearts, how mysterious his reactions were even to the disciples who were with him every day. Though others disdained and avoided the Samaritan woman, Jesus loved her (see John 4:9-10). He ate with people who were viewed as the worst kind of sinners (see Matthew 9:10-12). His very nature went against the grain and baffled the minds of those who thought they knew God. And in the end, the world mocked him when he mysteriously refused to come down from the cross and save himself from such great pain (see Luke 23:35). To our human natures, Jesus was and is a complete mystery—his actions, his words, his heart. Mystery was his way of living. And dying. But to our spiritual natures, this mystery is revealed as we seek to know him more (see Matthew 7:7).

It shouldn't be a surprise that our call as believers to imitate the life of Christ would also lead us to that same mystery that makes him so alluring, so different from the rest of the world. In 1 Corinthians 11:1, Paul calls believers to imitate Christ. Beautifully, mysteriously, as we accept Christ, we find ourselves in the possession of his Spirit. "The person who is joined to the Lord is one spirit with him" (1 Corinthians 6:17). As we accept the life of Christ and all the mystery that it entails, we also accept the mind of God himself. First Corinthians 2:16 states that "we understand these things, for we have the mind of Christ." Because of that, the imitation of Christ's life, and therefore his mystery, is within our reach as we walk this earth and relate to those who love us and those who hate us. Rather than thinking of Christ as a mystery we must solve, we must embrace his mystery, as it is this mystery that draws people to him in the first place.

This call to imitate the mystery of Christ is not a gentle request but a God-initiated command. Yet how many of us take the words of imitation seriously? At times my heart lacks the strength to stand, so it retreats into the habit of fear and worry, and looks nothing like the heart of Christ. I depart from the imitation of the God I love, and I travel to the land of introspection and anxiety. And the mystery is lost. It isn't until I look from the trials of life to the God who sustains me that I can reclaim the ground I lost. It is a daily returning. I confess my retreat, and I promise to march forward in faith and hope. "Day by day" has become my battle cry. My constant fight is against the conflicting impulses that tug at my heart and distract me from the face of God.

For a number of years, I struggled with a horrific fear of flying. I would see images of plane crashes on the news, and I couldn't get them out of my head. So each time I would get onto a plane, my heart would pound, my mind would race, and my gut would hurt. And although I didn't explode like I thought I would—and neither did the plane—I would end up physically sore, emotionally tired, and literally sickened by the end of each arduous flight.

Each time we landed, I would look back over my stressful trip and say to myself, *Why can't I trust God with my life?* I knew all the biblical responses. I coached people through their fears. But this fear controlled me. However, each time I wanted to give up flying altogether, I'd say, "No, I will not let fear, a sin, control me." And so I would fly in spite of the difficulty and stress of it. After much prayer and much refusal to let anything other than God control me, I am happy to say that I can now fly without fear. There are days in my life when I look like anything but a believer, let alone like Christ himself, but I refuse to let that be the end of me or define me. Instead, I push forward to attain what God promised me—the ability to imitate the life of peace and hope of Jesus himself.

No matter what your area of struggle is—whether it's failing to trust God with your fears, failing to keep the mystery alive, or failing to embrace his version of true romance—don't give up. I want to make it clear to your heart that perfection isn't attainable this side of glory. But the desire to imitate Christ is worth pursuing. As many times as we fall down, we can keep getting up and trying again.

Three Kinds of Romance

If you talked to a dozen women about what romance means, you'd likely get a dozen different answers. One woman might say it's getting red roses; another might say it has to be wildflowers. Some might say it's a mountain getaway; others might say it's Times Square at midnight. Or maybe a picnic by the lake is better than a candlelit dinner at a fancy restaurant. Opinions on what romance is may vary, so it might be best to establish what the term *romance* means to the Woman of Mystery. I believe there are actually three different kinds of romance: manufactured romance, earthly romance, and true romance. Manufactured romance and earthly romance are only imitations of true romance. They give us hints of its flavor but not the full taste.

Manufactured romance is the least genuine of the three. It is an attempt to force romance through setting and circumstances. It is the imitation romance of films and music. Manufactured romance is going to a chick flick in order to get a taste of romance for ourselves. It is opening a Pottery Barn catalog and believing that if we could just have *that* room, our lives would be magical. It's the romance we arrange ourselves when the real thing is lacking. And it's little more than a false high that leaves us feeling empty when the vision and the hope wear off.

Earthly romance is a closer imitation of the real thing. Not only can it peacefully coexist with true romance, but it can also amplify it. Earthly romance is that thing that happens between a man and a woman. It is the way the world fades into the background when you look into his eyes. It is that feeling that keeps you up at night with excitement and hope, and it is those moments when your heart feels truly adored and loved by one man who is wholly and completely devoted to you. And in its truest form, earthly romance is something God created to be a natural taste of the divine. But it can never be a substitute for true romance.

True romance is what all other forms of romance seek to imitate. It comes from a relationship with a holy God and is more amazing than any earthly relationship could ever be. It comes as you worship, as you obey, as you love. When your heart becomes aware of God's presence, feelings of peace, hope, joy, and even ecstasy can overtake you (see John 14:27). The world starts to look a little brighter and seem a little less harsh toward you (see Psalm 37:3-4). When your thoughts mirror God's thoughts, and when you can say that he is all you ever really want or need, then true romance descends upon you.

This is a romance that cannot be shaken, no matter how bad your outward circumstances. It stands in the face of every trial, every attack, and every heartache. It brings you tears of joy and real feelings of comfort and support. When you experience true romance, you know in the very center of your soul that you are loved with the kind of love that is beyond compare. And that love will never disappoint. It is this true romance that is the answer to all other longings for love in your life. Without true romance, earthly romance becomes fleeting and unsatisfying, but with it, all earthly romance is enhanced and strengthened. Gain true romance and you will never again need to ask, "Where is the romance?"

When I was single I had moments of despair. Would I ever find a man to love? Would I be alone forever? It was an emotional time. I can remember feeling deflated and wanting so badly to have someone hold me and say I was beautiful, to romance me and make me happy to be adored. But no one was to be found. In a lonely funk one evening, I walked out onto my porch, sat down to watch the sunset, and found just what I was looking for. The breeze gently touched my skin, and I sighed. The smell of fresh-cut grass made me inhale deeply. And the orange sky made me say thank you. How foolish I had been, looking for earthly romance when true romance was there right in front of me. Who needs flowers when you have a sunset designed by the very hand of the one who loves you most? Who needs a hug when his very creation fills your lungs and surrounds your body with every breath? When I pushed out my thoughts of what I lacked and focused on the abundance that was mine, I realized that true romance wasn't dependent on the presence or the lack of a man in my life.

When Jesus was nearing the end of his time here on earth, he offered us these words: "I am leaving you with a gift—peace of mind and heart. And the peace I give is a gift the world cannot give. So don't be troubled or afraid" (John 14:27). True romance is a gift the world cannot give. It is beyond compare, and it is available to everyone who seeks it. The Woman of Mystery is a woman who understands the secret to true romance and the need for it in her life. Because of her connection to God, she has an air of mystery that captivates those who are near her.

But becoming a Woman of Mystery can initially feel like a daunting task. Her qualities seem too perfect to be attained, her choices too impossible to imitate. I know from experience. I was not always a lover of mystery. I was an aggressive, successful executive type who took the world and the boardroom by the horns. I found it rewarding to shock people and to demand attention.

I can remember one particularly notable nonmysterious move that I once made that caused a few jaws to drop. I was presenting at an important sales meeting for the publisher I worked for. This conservative publishing house was, at the time, populated with middle-aged men who found me a bit of a wild card in the world of Bible publishing. In my belief that shocking people helped me to get my point across, I had chosen to wear an outfit that seemed to solicit a lot of comments. As I walked the length of the large—very large—mahogany conference table, the guys proceeded to make comic remarks about my attire. "You singing at a wedding later today?" They all laughed and murmured their snarky remarks. So, when I got to my seat at the head of the table surrounded by some thirty men, I put down my papers and pulled out my chair. Then I stepped up on it and onto the shiny wood table. "Take a good look!" I pronounced. "Have your laughs now. Get it out of your system." I twirled around slowly as they all sat in shock. As I came back around to face them, the huge doors at the other end of the conference room opened and the CEO of the company walked in. His very conservative jaw dropped, and a look of discomfort came over him. And I enjoyed every minute of it. Let's just say that on that day I made my mark on the company.

Lest you think as you read this book that I'm now a quiet church-lady type and that mystery comes naturally to me, let me assure you that I am the exact opposite. I am, at heart, a driven, assertive woman who is at times both a social hermit and a show woman. When I'm expected to perform, I am the center of attention and take command of the crowd. But when I'm not on, I am shy by nature and would rather spend my days at home alone than with crowds of people. I can tell you that my desire to achieve has often made me do things even I am shocked by, both in the boardroom and in the romantic world. Most of the time, I've gotten it all wrong.

My dating life spanned almost two decades. And over those years I made many mistakes. For most of my adult life, I was the aggressor, not only in business, but also in love. I chased men, argued with them, and baffled them. I can't tell you how many men said, "Can you just stop being the man in this relationship?" And for years I couldn't understand what they were talking about and why I was still single. I was a catch! (Isn't that what we all tell ourselves?) Even after I got married, remnants of my "masculine" tendencies remained. But more on that later. It wasn't until after I started to discover the power of mystery that I was set free from this constant state of internal unrest. I was no longer striving or pushing against the world. I was living in step with it and the people around me, and I was finding beauty where I had never seen it before. I'm far from the picture of perfect mystery, but I'm miles closer than I used to be.

And so when I talk about this woman that we aspire to become, know that I have yet to get it all right. But as I embark on this life of mystery, I'm finding it is not only more relationally rewarding but more spiritually rewarding as well. I hope that these words resonate with you and that you will risk testing them to see if they are true. May this be a chance for you to find your heart full of true romance and the love that goes along with it.

Lifting the Veil

FINDING ROMANCE

Don't look for more candles or romantic music; try to look for opportunities to admire, even adore, God's creation. And that includes your husband, if you have one, as well as your friends and family. Find the good in everything from nature to smells to tastes, and you will begin to discover the romance. Spend time each day taking it all in. Meditate on the goodness in your life; disregard the negative. Refuse to become a slave to resenting what God himself has given you. And major on the positives.

ROMANTIC INVENTORY

Take a look at your life over the past five to ten years. What are some of the most romantic moments you've had? What has made them so romantic? What about the times romance was lacking? How did you handle its absence? Can you think of some ways you could replace those longings with God himself? Spend some time in prayer and Bible study, finding out how to fall deeper in love with Jesus.

WORSHIP MUSIC

I have found that if I listen to my favorite uplifting music while reading devotional and other inspirational books, I increase the degree of understanding and penetration to my heart. It's the sound track of life, as I like to call it. So I encourage you to pick up your iPod or turn on the CD player and allow the sound track of life to add to the experience of reading and absorbing this book and other books you're reading.

her Essence

Prince Henry: "You told me it was a matter of life or death."

Leonardo da Vinci: "A woman always is, sire."
• EVER AFTER

I know that she is good and strong and deserves all the love this world
has to give. Can't you see that, how wonderful, how special she is?
• A WALK IN THE CLOUDS

It is the dim haze of mystery that adds enchantment to pursuit.
• ANTOINE RIVAROL

The mystery of romance is found in your very essence. When a
man desires to reach to the sky for you and pull down a star, it's
because of your essence. When he would swim the English Channel in order to win your heart, it's because of who you are at your
very core. When he would fight off any enemy on your behalf, it's
because of the value he sees in you. Your essence is who you are,
not how you look. It is what you think, how you feel, and what
you believe. And it expresses itself effortlessly, even silently. It is
what makes you distinctly you—and it is what makes him either
adore you or run from you. It's that thing that says to his heart,
There is chemistry here, or *I want to know more about this person.* It is

what keeps him talking and what brings him back for more. Most people can sense another's essence within the first few minutes of meeting. In fact, most men say they know within the first fifteen minutes of meeting a woman if they will fall in love with her.

Call it essence or chemistry, but it affects how people interact and who they choose to be with. And that is why when a man first meets the woman whose heart he wants to capture, he often becomes either boastful or entertaining. He boasts because, like a man sitting down for an important interview, he wants to make a good impression. He wants you to see his strengths, his ability to earn a living, his character, his muscles, and all that defines him as a man. If he is witty, then he wants you to find value in his charm and his ability to make you laugh. If he is smart, then he wants you to admire his intelligence. When a man finds an essence in a woman that gives him strength and tells him this could be someone worth fighting for, he determines to go to great lengths to capture her heart. And that is when romance first gets its start. When a man pursues a woman, that is his attempt to prove to her that she is of great value to him.

Many men create elaborate plans to prove their love. They spend more money than they should on flowers, limousines, dinners, and other expressions of love. I can remember one guy I dated who would come to my house every weekend and work in my yard with me. He took care of my home as if it were his own, all in an attempt to prove his love. A man will work with all his strength to show a woman how much he wants her and wants to provide for her. And the heart of a woman responds when a man finds it beautiful and worthy of such affection and care.

At those moments, those romantic moments, you just might

get a better glimpse into the woman God created you to be. When a man finds something within you that drives him to express his love, your heart is lifted and you are strengthened by hope (see Proverbs 13:12). And because of that hope, you have the ability to more clearly see your value. Romance is not ordinary behavior for a man. His typical actions suddenly come to a halt, and he begins to behave as if the object of his affection is the only thing important in all the world. And for a woman, this is exhilarating. To think that another human being would offer such devotion, such honor, such courage just to win her love is an amazing feeling. And it confirms to her heart that she is indeed of great value.

When a man is willing to go to great lengths to prove his love for you—even to die, if that's what it takes—you can be sure that a great romance is in the air. You may have never felt that kind of romantic love. Such a mystery has perhaps never unfolded around you, but even if it hasn't, my hunch is that there's something inside you that believes someday it will. If you've tasted romance and found that it is good, then no doubt you're continually seeking more. I know that I have had several tastes from the romantic well, and I have fallen.

If romance has eluded you or even left a bitter taste in your mouth, my guess is that you still haven't given up on romance entirely. But if you have written off romance, then I'm going to ask you to reconsider for a moment and ask yourself if it was *true* romance or an imitation that tainted you. Think about whether you believe that true romance with your Savior could have the power to change your heart, to give you another chance at the romance you used to believe in. I believe that romance is available to all of us, even those of us who have failed more times than we can count or who have yet to ever experience it. Because romance doesn't rely solely on a man to provide it or on your own ability to generate it.

So the big question that must be asked is, What creates romance? Is it something external—the perfect Pottery Barn–furnished room with the mingled smells of new leather and fresh flowers to give you just the right feeling? Is it the candlelit dance floor with the romantic music and the perfect little black dress? Is romance dependent on the initiative of the man who offers it? Or does the creation of romance have something to do with *you*?

The Essence of True Romance

The real question is, Is there a formula you can use to manufacture romance anytime you want it? Or is it more elusive than that—something that has a life of its own and requires two hearts to be in sync before anything can happen? Well, the answer is twofold. Earthly romance between a man and a woman does require the difficult equation of two hearts beating to the same rhythm. It requires agreement. If one attempts to attain earthly romance while the other isn't thinking romantic thoughts, all will be foiled. And that's what makes that kind of romance so elusive: it takes two. But there is another romance—a romance that is less transitory and requires only the commitment of your heart in order to unfold. That is because the other heart involved in this true romance is already committed, already in love and willing to give all of himself to bring you joy. This true romance is the romance that is being offered to you right this very minute, wherever you are.

It is the romance of a lifetime, and it is the foundation for all earthly romance that you will ever desire. With true romance in sight, earthly romance becomes more readily available, even when circumstances seem to war against it. In the true romance equation, there *is* someone who would die for you. He would give up everything for you. And he would be everything, just to win your heart. He is the author of true romance, and his heart has created within you a craving to love and be loved. When your heart comes into contact with this kind of romance, you are impacted down to your very essence. It colors you. It remakes you—your heart, your spirit, and your emotions. It makes the very heart of who you are more peaceful and content, and therefore more attractive. True romance not only offers *your* heart the love it craves; it also offers the same thing to the man you have been given (or one day may be given). Because on the wings of true romance, your heart can soar to new heights of respect and admiration, and out of that comes a feeling of love that any man would cherish.

There was a time in my life when I had only manufactured romance. I had never experienced true romance, so I tried to generate an imitation of it. I would have fleeting moments of success when I would create a romantic environment and begin to feel lifted up, hopeful, even beautiful and desirable. But the moments of failure were much more familiar—moments when I would work to experience the romantic mood I craved, only to feel the sting of letdown once it ended. Then the feelings of emptiness and loneliness would kick in even stronger. I can remember spending hours in my bathtub with candles in every corner, bubbles up to my nose, and the most romantic music I could find playing in the background. I did everything I could to decorate the moment with the prospect of romance should someone ever find me beautiful at some point in the future. I remember the tears, the hopes that one day he would find me. I remember watching the movie *The Saint*, starring Val Kilmer. As a spy, his life was full of intrigue and danger, so when he met his leading lady, their lives became a wild adventure. He fought for her, rescued her, and loved her. She helped him, protected him, and loved him. And at the end of the movie, as they made their rendezvous at a secluded cottage in the woods, I sighed deeply. When the credits started rolling, the romance I had been a part of left me. And as I walked to my car, I remember having feelings of regret and sadness. I envied their love and his devotion and strength. Their romance. I was angry that the girl on the screen wasn't me. I was sad because that man hadn't sat down at a table next to mine and serendipitously knocked over my coffee, leading him to find me—his everything. I envied those who found what I longed for, and in the end I spiraled into a depression so deep that at one point I even dreamed of killing myself. Would no one ever find me valuable enough to give his all for me?

Then at the age of twenty-seven I found him. He had been there all along—I was just too focused on my manufactured romance to see true romance standing right in front of me. When I opened my old Bible that night, my eyes welled up and tears poured down my face. I had just lost my job, my boyfriend, and my hope. I was a new believer and knew very little of the strength of God or my faith in him. And so I drew my traditional bath and poured myself into it with two pieces of worn leather between my hands. Every word spoke to my heart. It was as if it had been written just for me, and it offered me a different kind of romance—a kind of love I never knew existed. I can remember reading two particular verses that spoke romance to my heart. They were the promises: "I will never fail you. I will never abandon you" (Hebrews 13:5) and "'I know the plans I have for you,' declares the LORD, 'plans to prosper you and not to harm you, plans to give you hope and a future'" (Jeremiah 29:11, NIV). At that point I was Christ's— hook, line, and sinker. Unabashedly in love. And that's when the romance began.

But over time, like all romances have a tendency to do, the intensity of my love weakened. I got comfortable with him, and soon the tears of overwhelming joy gave way to a comfortable familiarity. It wasn't long before I started looking for romance in different places again. In my rationalization, I wasn't doing this to replace him but to supplement my emotional need to feel valuable and worthwhile. I went back to manufactured romance—chick flicks, romantic music, anything that would placate my need for love. And I did have moments of romance, but they were precarious and fleeting, dependent on my emotional state and my ability to suspend the moment.

It wasn't until much later that I learned how to bring true romance back into my heart and earthly romance back into my love life. All this time, even after encountering true romance, I thought that earthly romance was entirely the responsibility of the man who would offer it. I wasn't aware of my role in it, other than being willing to prepare the environment and my wardrobe. I didn't know I could affect it. Now I see that the lifting of my heart, the appreciation of the colors that surround me and the sounds that entice me, and the value of the man in front of me have more to do with me and my essence than with anything else. True romance is the result of a heart that is open to the voice and hand of our loving God, which in turn affects our essence. And it is the result of our willingness to find truth even in the hard moments, to see his hand in every situation and his love in everything that comes into our lives. When a woman can muster the strength to be open and willing, her essence will be so colored and changed that everyone around her will find hope in her presence.

Her Essence Is Confident

God calls us to a life of faith—faith that he is God and we are not, and that he offers us all we need to be complete and satisfied. It is this confidence that creates in you a mystery that draws a world of true romance to its side. And incidentally, it is this confidence in who you are, because of who God is, that is so alluring to a man. I believe there is a difference between self-confidence and God-confidence. Self-confidence often scares men off. Before I met Jesus, I was very self-confident with men, and I scared off plenty with my assertive and even aggressive nature. I gave men little mystery to discover and few nuances to explore, because my self-confidence sought to prove itself and assert itself in every situation. But once I made the gradual change from focusing on confidence in myself to focusing on confidence in who God is, I became more comfortable with who I was, more comfortable to be around. I ceased my striving to be seen and heard, and I relaxed in the knowledge that I didn't need these things from a man; I only needed to be seen and heard by my God.

On the opposite end of the spectrum of confidence is insecurity and self-loathing. Both are mystery-defeating. They repel others from your presence. Insecurity makes kind people feel uncomfortable and nasty people feel disinterested or just plain aggressive.

When a woman is confident in her relationship with God, she is not only more of a mystery to the opposite sex but also more selective. A confident woman doesn't thrive on rejection or abuse. She might have to convince her heart through continually reading God's Word and denying those old recordings that play over and over again in her head, but she knows that she deserves just as much love as she is willing to give.

The story goes that long ago a man in a village was looking for a wife. There was a woman in the town whom everyone thought was homely and would never find a man. But when this man saw her, he knew she was the one for him. In that particular village, a man was expected to offer something of equal value for the bride he chose. And so the acceptable gift to the father of a young woman might be a cow or two, or maybe a pig and a chicken, depending on the perceived value of the woman in question. The father of this homely young woman believed that he would be lucky to get a couple of chickens for his daughter. So imagine his surprise when the young man came to town and offered him five cows for his daughter. This was a sum unequaled in their village. At first the father doubted the man's offer, but sure enough, the man showed up the next day with five cows. The entire family was overjoyed, but their joy was nothing compared to the heart of the girl whose value was being displayed for all to see. That evening she married the handsome stranger, and the next morning those who saw her said her beauty was beyond compare. This once homely girl was suddenly valued far above all the other women, and she began to shine. There was no longer anything ugly about her. Her entire countenance had changed. Sure, she was the same young woman, but confidence had gifted her with beauty. And everyone around her could see it.

You might not ever be offered five cows for your love (everyone should be so lucky!), but be assured that you have been paid for with far more than livestock. You were made for a very great purpose: to love and to serve the Lord of lords. Confidence is being convinced that "you must love the LORD your God with all your heart, all your soul, all your mind, and all your strength" (Mark 12:30). If your soul obsession is not yourself nor the love of a man nor your need for romance, but God, then there is little room left in your heart or mind for insecurity, self-loathing, or fear.

Confidence Accepts What God Gives

You must know that the Creator didn't make a mistake when he made you. You may have moments when you think he did things wrong when he got to you, but God never messes up. Everything about you is made divinely in his image. The cut of your nose, the breadth of your hips, the family you were born into, and the longings of your heart were all initiated by God himself, and all it takes to make the world see the beauty in you is trust—not in yourself but in the God who created you. We all have weaknesses and areas in our lives where we are lacking, but God helps us work with those things, bringing them into line with his Word. He promises to help burn off the impurities and leave only the finest gold.

All of us as women have something we could be unhappy with when it comes to our bodies, our personalities, our life circumstances. But the secret is acceptance of things we can't change, which manifests itself in contentment. Contentment is simply a steady knowledge that God is ultimately in control of everything that has been given to us. "Whatever is good and perfect comes down to us from God our Father, who created all the lights in the heavens. He never changes or casts a shifting shadow. He chose to give birth to us by giving us his true word. And we, out of all creation, became his prized possession" (James 1:17-18). And because you are his prized possession—his love, the object of his true romance—he knows what is best for you. Acceptance understands this and takes everything that comes as a gift, not a torment. Certainly things will happen that were meant for evil in a fallen world, but God promises to use even those things for good (see Romans 8:28). When you start to believe that nothing happens to you except what God can and will use for your benefit, then you can learn to accept everything as a way to draw closer to the true romance God has for you.

Confidence Is Not Self-Esteem

Confidence is not self-esteem. It isn't having a high regard for yourself—knowing you can do it all on your own, or make it through on sheer willpower, or pull yourself up by your own bootstraps. Self-esteem is for people who are their own greater power. But the Woman of Mystery knows that when she is weak, he is strong (see 2 Corinthians 12:9-10). She knows that no matter how much she might fail or what turmoil she may be feeling, he is constant. If you are looking for self-esteem to make you confident, you are looking in the wrong

"My grace is all you need. My power works best in weakness." So now I am glad to boast about my weaknesses, so that the power of Christ can work through me. That's why I take pleasure in my weaknesses, and in the insults, hardships, persecutions, and troubles that I suffer for Christ. For when I am weak, then I am strong.

2 Corinthians 12:9-10

place, because self disappoints, but God never does. You would be wiser to seek God-esteem rather than an esteem built on who you are or what you've done. There is both freedom and confidence in the knowledge that hope and happiness don't rest in your hands but in the hands of the one who holds the world. The confidence that is available for everyone is a confidence in the perfection of God and not of self. That should be a relief to us. We don't have to look for salvation in our actions or in our strength of will but in the God who saves all who trust in him (see Acts 4:12). This kind of confidence is not only unshakable but also self-sacrificing, selfless, and compassionate (see John 15:13). When you esteem God and his ways more highly than yourself, you have everything you need (see 2 Corinthians 5:14-15).

Finding Confidence

Nothing is more attractive than confidence. And if it isn't in you, then start to look upward. Put your confidence in the God who created you and loves you. Trust his hand in your life, and your confidence will shine through. And then you will begin to find the secret to the Woman of Mystery in you. In a practical sense, the best way I've found to do this is to take my eyes off of myself every morning. Each day, before the rest of the house wakes up, I open up my computer and study my God. I journal on my laptop while I pray, and I have a virtual seminary library on my hard drive to study and gain inspiration from. I start out each session with adoration—telling God how amazing he is. And as I do that, my load lifts. I start to verbally confirm his majesty and power. And since our minds tend to believe what they hear from our lips, I am calmed. I stop considering life from my perspective and start to see it from a more heavenly vantage point. After that I confess every-thing I did wrong the previous day. At first this was a daunting task—how could I have such a huge list of sins? I was never so keenly aware of them as when I started confessing daily. And then it was embarrassing. It can take some time to run the laundry list of mess-ups and spiritual disappointments, believe me. But week by week it gets easier, as confession reminds your thoughts and heart what is really important and who's really in charge. Confidence grows as you start to use your voice to remember who God is and what you aren't: perfect.

I remember a time when a pastor told me, "Hayley, you have to stop playing God." I was shocked by his words—I'd never considered that I had a God complex. But then I saw it. Each time I worried excessively about taking care of people, protecting them, or fixing them, I took on the role of God. I made their mental, emotional, and even spiritual health my problem. And while this should be your role to some degree when it comes to your children, it sure isn't your role with your coworkers, friends, boyfriend, or husband. Letting go of the idea that the ultimate well-being of others rests on you not only is freeing but also helps you to put your confidence in the right place—in the strength of God instead of yourself.

Confidence rests not in your knowledge of your perfection but in your knowledge of his.

Men are drawn to confidence like a moth to a flame—in part because of what confidence offers them. A confident woman isn't overly needy and doesn't put a strain on a man to be something to her that he cannot be. Instead, he finds something in her that is mutually beneficial and makes both their lives more enjoyable and enriching. What's left out of that old saying about the moth is that if it gets too close to the flame, it is destroyed by the very thing it seeks! So a careful balance between confidence and humility is the best thing for a woman—and for the man in her life.

> *It is not a question of giving up sin, but of giving up my right to myself, my natural independence and self-assertiveness, and this is where the battle has to be fought. . . . Beware of refusing to go to the funeral of your own independence. The natural life is not spiritual, and it can only be made spiritual by sacrifice.*
>
> — OSWALD CHAMBERS

Her Essence Is Humble

In our modern world of celebrity worship and self-promotion, humility often carries with it a negative image. But when Christ became human and took on the sins of the world, he showed us a beautiful image of humility (see Philippians 2:6-8). Humility is not self-loathing, it is not bitterness clothed in martyrdom, and it is not weakness. Instead it is "an ungrudging and unhypocritical acknowledgment of absolute dependence upon God" (*Tyndale Bible Dictionary*). Humility says, "I am unworthy, and he is worthy;

I agree that I am the worst of sinners, and I thank God for grace, because boy do I need it" (see 1 Timothy 1:15). Humility is the opposite of pride, and that is where the beauty lies.

It is often thought that humility simply means admitting our utter sinfulness and dependence on God's divine forgiveness. And while that is obviously a part of it, it is not the whole story. For if it were, then Christ would not have been described as humble, because he had no sin in need of forgiveness. Clearly Christ's humility is a characteristic that has to do with his goodness and selflessness rather than acknowledgment of sin. In our world, humility is both rare and beautiful. And it echoes the humility of Christ to a world that's hungry for authenticity and acceptance. When we live in the humility of Christ, we give up our right to fight for the wants and needs we are told we so clearly deserve. We become more interested in serving God and loving those around us than in being heard, understood, and recognized ourselves. When a woman lives in this kind of humility, she draws out the curiosity of a man. Not only is he interested in what makes her tick, but he is also inspired by her willingness to admit when she is wrong and to look beyond herself to invest in the lives and dreams of others. Humility becomes her.

Humble might not be the first word a man would use to describe his perfect woman, but the actions that spring from her humility reveal her character to him. He might not be able to put it into words, but acts of humility are attractive in a woman. And humility shows itself in the life of the Woman of Mystery when she makes an effort to be kind to people who can't do a thing for her in return. Humility finds something lovely in everyone. It isn't judgmental or prideful; it is full of acceptance and love.

Without some intentionality, it's easy to ignore strangers, people who are serving you, or even those who are interrupting you. It's tempting to assign to them less value by becoming angry with them or treating them as less important than yourself. But that is both unbiblical and unattractive. The command to "clothe yourselves with tenderhearted mercy, kindness, humility, gentleness, and patience" (Colossians 3:12) leaves us no room to be careless toward those in our paths.

A man often wonders, especially near the beginning of a relationship, *How will she treat me when I don't please her?* If you order people around as if they are your servants, he is no doubt taking note. But when you are conscious of those who wait on you and when you care about them as human beings, your essence begins to glow. We do this for one audience only: the God who showed us kindness himself. But a side benefit is that people notice too, including the man in your life.

> **Humility** is a socially acknowledged claim to neutrality in the competition of life.
>
> HARPER'S BIBLE DICTIONARY

By nature I am very shy until I see something that I really want or need. And then I become assertive—fearless, even—in voicing my needs, concerns, and opinions. Which might make me a good advocate or negotiator, but it can also make me a miserable customer and human being. There was a time when I believed that a woman should ask for exactly what she wants and that those who are paid to serve her should do just that: serve. And so my common practice was this: Upon arriving at a restaurant, I would immediately ask for a booth. As the host or hostess took us through the restaurant, I would point out the exact location I wanted. I believed in asking for what I wanted, after all. Then after sitting down to order, I was the high-maintenance woman. "Can I get some lemon for my water? Can you adjust the thermostat? It's cold in here. Would you have them take off the onions and the lettuce and add cheese and mushrooms, but could they cook them really, really well so that the food is almost burned?" And the list would go on and on. It wasn't until I went to dinner with another high-maintenance woman that I felt the sting of being the ugly customer. I started to recognize how unattractive it was to order the servers around as if they were somehow less than human and had time for me and me alone.

How we treat others around us—friends as well as strangers—tells the men with us a lot about our hearts and ultimately about how much we are capable of obeying God's command to love others as we love ourselves. In his letter to the Philippians, Paul makes it clear that we must "in humility count others more significant than yourselves" (Philippians 2:3, ESV). Though I admit that it takes effort not to be difficult, I am working on asking for things with gentleness, and I make every effort to treat those who serve me as human beings by talking to them about their days and asking them their names. I try to consider others before myself, and one of the payoffs, in addition to knowing this is pleasing to God, has been an air about me that makes my husband proud. And in those moments of looking for beauty in everyone, in seeing them as children of God, I find a taste of the true romance I knew when I first met the Father. And I am uplifted to a new vantage point, where romance becomes more and more possible, whether or not it comes in the traditional form of flowers and chocolate.

Her Essence Is Hopeful

In your very essence you were created to be hopeful. We are reminded by Paul to "be joyful in hope, patient in affliction, faithful in prayer" (Romans 12:12, NIV). But perhaps all hope left you long ago after much disappointment. Maybe your father left you or your mother hates you. Maybe your friend betrayed you or the world has rejected you. Regardless of how it happened, hope has deserted you. And now you are left with the cold, harsh reality of your emptiness, fear, and worry. But you were not made for such emotions. You were created to hope. And God's presence in your life is meant to be all the hope you need. Like all other healthy emotions, hope isn't dependent on your circumstances but on God's power. Perhaps you can take heart, as I have, in these words: "In our hearts we felt the sentence of death. But this happened that we might not rely on ourselves but on God, who raises the dead. He has delivered us from such a deadly peril, and he will deliver us. On him we have set our hope that he will continue to deliver us" (2 Corinthians 1:9-10, NIV).

Hope is available for anyone who has faith in God: "Faith is being sure of what we hope for and certain of what we do not see" (Hebrews 11:1, NIV). Hope defines faith; without hope, there is no faith. If you believe, then you have some degree of hope left in you. So turn to what you believe in—a God who delivers, a truth that never disappoints, and a faith that is founded on that hope—and you will find what you need.

To grow or restore the hope, first transfer the location of your hope from people to God. "Lord, where do I put my hope? My only hope is in you" (Psalm 39:7). People will always disappoint. They weren't meant to be our hope, so it is no wonder that hope starts to disappear when it is placed where it cannot grow. When you, like others before you, tell God, "I am worn out waiting for your rescue," you must complete that thought and say, "but I have put my hope in your word" (Psalm 119:81). Because it is through the gift of God's Word that you can find the hope promised you. Hope is found when you open your Bible and start to read it. In his Word you can find the answers you need, the love you crave, and the assurance that everything that has happened to you cannot destroy you but only draws you closer to the Comforter. "We can rejoice, too, when we run into problems and trials, for we know that they help us develop endurance. And endurance develops strength of character, and character strengthens our confident hope of salvation. And this hope will not lead to disappointment. For we know how dearly God loves us, because he has given us the Holy Spirit to fill our hearts with his love" (Romans 5:3-5).

Hope is an uplifting emotion, not only for the woman who believes in its power, but also for the man who witnesses it. Your hope is evidence of your faith; it is a firm belief that God is good and that he will never disappoint. Women who offer hope to the man in their lives offer the very breath of God. They give him strength and a hope of his own.

Hope, even in the face of opposition and failure, is the fuel for romance, because it drives a man to attempt everything he can in order to not disappoint the one who believes in him. The mystery of hope is that it can be found even when there is no earthly evidence to support it. Whether it feels this way or not right now, you have the ability within you to be hopeful, no matter what the circumstances. Life is always one grand adventure after another for the woman who lives with hope.

her Essence

Think of your favorite romantic movie. Undoubtedly, toward the end of the movie there is a moment of crisis—a moment when it looks as if all is lost. And even in the midst of that misery and apparent failure, as you watch from your comfortable stadium seat, you have hope. You feel for the heroine—you may even cry for her—but deep down you have hope. Even if the movie ends without the satisfaction of a happy ending, you find in her suffering a grandness, an adventure that is not only entertaining but also rich with life and, yes, maybe even hope. It's easy to remain expectant when we watch the lives of others (especially the likes of movie heroines, who always get the perfect guy and usually the happy ending). When it comes to our lives, though, we don't have the guarantee of a Hollywood ending, and we can quickly lose hope. But have you ever taken a look at your life as if it were a movie unraveling before your eyes? This is something that has worked well for me. I drink in the good and the bad and live it all to my core, and I can always be hopeful, even confident, that the happy ending is coming. And even if it doesn't come as I imagine, it will come in a better way still.

I firmly believe that the great Scriptwriter has a better ending in store for me than I could ever come up with myself. After all, Scripture confirms that he is able to "accomplish infinitely more than we might ask or think" (Ephesians 3:20). I might not see the happy ending this side of heaven, but heaven is fast approaching. And I know what I will find there: "Because of his grace he declared us righteous and gave us confidence that we will inherit eternal life" (Titus 3:7). It is because of this that I enjoy life so much. Every future episode is a book waiting to be written, a movie wanting to be filmed. And when I think of my life in terms of others

The Source of *Hopelessness*

~ believing circumstances define you

~ deciding hope comes only from eventually getting what you want

~ failing to retreat to the comfort of God's Word

~ seeing suffering as something destructive instead of something valuable

~ taking your eyes off of the spiritual side of things

~ distrusting or hating yourself more than you trust or love God

~ believing you are too tough of a case for God to care about

The Source of *Hope*

~ spending time meditating on God and his Word

~ believing strongly that God is in control even when it looks like he isn't

~ refusing to believe you need anything more than air, food, water, shelter, and God himself

~ taking your eyes off of your circumstances and placing them on God

~ trusting God's grace to be enough for you

~ allowing suffering to do its work and help you develop endurance, strength of character, and hope

~ knowing that your faith in God, not what happens to you, defines you

viewing it and finding the underlying story of a life in the hands of a good God, I relax and enjoy, even in the hard moments. God offers romance in the little, unexpected things in life, and it's only my inability to reach out and accept it that keeps it from my grasp. So I want to reach out and grab hold of the romance in everything. And suddenly the world around me softens. The screaming child becomes a comedy of errors and not a battle of anger and frustration. The irritating husband or coworker becomes a tool in the Carpenter's hand suited just for me, made to smooth my rough edges and make me more into the woman I am called to be.

And so this is what I aspire to live by: "When troubles come your way, consider it an opportunity for great joy. For you know that when your faith is tested, your endurance has a chance to grow. So let it grow, for when your endurance is fully developed, you will be perfect and complete, needing nothing" (James 1:2-4).

Her Essence Is Joyful

If you look to the world around you for joy, you will come up lacking. If you look to the man in front of you for joy, he will disappoint you at one point or another. If you look to yourself for joy, you will find that you can't conjure up something that isn't there. That's normal. When joy depends on things and people, it is a temporary emotion, often referred to as happiness. Happiness is a wonderful thing and a goal of most every woman I know. But what happens when there is no trigger for happiness—when nothing is working right, no one is cooperating, and everything is hard? Where do you find your strength, your joy, that unwavering happiness that doesn't depend on circumstance? How do you capture it, tame it, and make it your own?

her Essence

Even though I know I shouldn't, many times I subconsciously agree with the world's definition of happiness. The world says you can't be happy if you don't have what you want. And I most often agree. Get what I want: happiness. Get what I don't want: anger and frustration, not joy. It's almost instinct for me. I've seen it so much in magazines and on talk shows—statements about what a woman deserves, what she needs to be whole and happy. I've been fed this lie so often that I actually find it to be a part of my very fiber. So when things don't go my way, I resent it. "Every person I know gets a vacation. They get rest, but I get a working vacation. How fair is that? I need some time on a beach somewhere to recharge!" I complain. The longer I think about what I lack, the more my resentment turns to frustration and then to anger. I'm cut off by a nasty driver, and I explode. I don't get the perfect romantic reaction from my husband, and I melt down. I think about everything my life is lacking, and I become bitter and resentful. When things don't go my way, those reactions suddenly start feeling like acceptable sins.

But sin should never get a pass, even when it seems justified, even when the world has given me the short end of the stick. Even when I'm right and they are all wrong, sin is still sin. And the truth is that sin steals joy. God is the author of joy, and joy is his gift to us (see Ecclesiastes 2:26). So when I sin and turn away from him, how can I expect to get the gift he is waiting to hand to me?

I have found that my lack of joy firmly rests on my inability to consistently agree with God. Instead of relying on him for joy and hope, I tend to look to my earthly circumstances to satisfy me. In the words of Oswald Chambers, it is this "subtle irritability caused by giving too much thought to our circumstances" that cuts off our joy.

How did Jesus find joy in his life? And how did he maintain that joy when he was laboring so hard and when he knew that the pain of the Cross was to come? His joy came through his total surrender and self-sacrifice, which were grounded in the firm knowledge that all he needed to do was fulfill the will of God. "Because of the joy awaiting him, he endured the cross, disregarding its shame" (Hebrews 12:2). When our joy is threatened, when people irritate and situations deflate, we can imitate Jesus' example. "Think of all the hostility he endured from sinful people; then you won't become weary and give up. After all, you have not yet given your lives in your struggle against sin" (Hebrews 12:3-4). Joy is found in doing the will of God, not in getting everything right or even in getting everything good.

Maybe you believe that joy isn't something you can just turn on or off. And that makes sense. Emotions can't always be controlled. So then why would God command us to be joyful? Why does James tell us to "consider it an opportunity for great joy" when troubles come our way (James 1:2)? And why does Paul say, "Always be full of joy in the Lord. I say it again—rejoice!" (Philippians 4:4)? No one can command you to feel something—to be giddy or depressed. So how can you be joyful in the midst of sorrow and suffering? The answer must be that joy isn't an emotion that precedes an action but an action that precedes an emotion. Practically speaking, that must mean that the path to joy looks like this: changing your attitude, changing your focus, and then changing the way you talk about what is in front of you. When you use words of joy and hope, eventually true joy will follow.

Obsessions—those things that you feel like you just have to have in order to be happy—are the biggest joy stealers around.

One of my biggest obsessions is comfort. When I go on vacation, I like to be pampered. I like nice rooms, good food, and peace and quiet. So when Michael and I went somewhere to get away and we found that nothing had been done to the room since 1971 and it smelled like smoke, I wanted to walk right back out and demand a better room. But then I stopped myself and thought, *Seriously, you can't be happy until you have what you imagined you should have? Or the best of what they can offer? Would Jesus complain about the room? Would he reject what was offered and demand something better? What makes me think I deserve anything in the first place? I betray God every day with my sinful choices. Why can't I, today, right now, choose to deny myself this pleasure of complaining and instead learn the secret of being content in any situation?* And as I asked myself these questions, as I worked through my so-called "needs," I found the joy in the situation. As it turned out, that ended up being one of our best vacations, and I'm not sure that would have happened if I had started it off with a list of complaints.

In God's economy, it isn't the luxury of the room or even the cleanliness of our surroundings that should bring us joy. True happiness comes from the hand of God in our lives and the complete acceptance that whatever he gives us is the best thing we could ever have. When you believe this, you can find joy in any circumstance.

Joy says that no matter what the situation—no matter who rejects me, fails me, or hurts me—I will still be fine, joyful even. Because no one but God can supply my joy. When a woman has a constant air of joy within her, a man is drawn to her. He finds her easy to be with and therefore a joy to be around. This doesn't mean she puts on a happy mask and pretends nothing is wrong when she's legitimately hurting. But it does mean that underneath the sadness, she is filled with an inexpressible assurance that life is good. And even if it isn't at the moment, this too shall pass. "After you have suffered a little while, he will restore, support, and strengthen you, and he will place you on a firm foundation" (1 Peter 5:10).

When a woman can find joy in her life and show it to those around her, people are drawn to the mystery and beauty of how she is able to rise above her circumstances, how she shines in every situation, how she trusts God with her every need. And she does this to draw people not to herself but to the Savior. I have not achieved all this by any stretch of the imagination, let's be clear. But it is my goal to choose joy instead of despair, to rejoice instead of worry. And even though I fail, I continue to get back up again and move toward my goal.

Her Essence Is Strength

The emotional life of a woman is both attractive and frightening to the man who stares into it. He is intrigued by her ability to feel so deeply, and he is touched by her heart. But when she has a heart that isn't working in tandem with her mind, she can easily become hurt by others or swayed from what she knows is right. The Woman of Mystery finds a way to see through people's words or actions in a particular situation. This allows her to see the truth and not to be hurt as easily. When you are easily hurt, you give much power to the perpetrator of the pain. And no one besides God himself should have such power over us. "I trust in God, so why should I be afraid? What can mere mortals do to me?" (Psalm 56:11). While you can't heal from a wound that you don't acknowledge, you have to be sure the acknowledgment of it is not the end but the beginning. Jesus reminds us, "Don't be afraid of those who want to kill your body; they cannot touch your soul. Fear only God, who can destroy both soul and body in hell" (Matthew 10:28).

A man is relieved when he finds a strong woman, one who isn't easily crushed by the words and actions of others. Certainly we all feel pain, we experience the hurt for a time, and we get bruised, but God gives us the strength to move past the pain and not remain stuck in it.

One such woman who stood strong against the evil of the world was Corrie ten Boom, who lived in Holland during World War II. After the Nazis discovered she was harboring Jews behind a secret wall in her bedroom, she was arrested and put into a concentration camp with her sister, Betsie. But instead of giving in to the horrors of Ravensbruck, they spent the evenings in worship. Women of all nationalities would crowd into a central area of the barracks, causing the bunks to groan under the weight. They sang praises in hushed voices. They read the Bible in one language, and then the words would be translated into several other languages as they made their way across the room. And with each breath, those frail, battered women found hope. They found a reason to press on and a reason to live. Corrie called those evenings beneath the lightbulb "little previews of heaven." Her sister, Betsie, died without tasting freedom from the camp, but before she passed away, she encouraged Corrie with these words: "[We] must tell them what we have learned here. We must tell them that there is no pit so deep that He is not deeper still. They will listen to us, Corrie, because we have been here." Both of these women relied on the strength God gave them and refused to let the evil of others define the essence of their lives. And even now, almost seven decades later, the mystery of God shines through their story.

Her Essence Is Forgiving

The Woman of Mystery seeks forgiveness, not revenge. It's so easy to want to retaliate when someone hurts us. I know my gut response to an attack is to fight back. I am a woman who is quick with words and ready to attack when I feel slighted, but I know that is not the standard God calls us to. We are instructed to "never take revenge. Leave that to the righteous anger of God. For the Scriptures say, 'I will take revenge; I will pay them back,' says the LORD" (Romans 12:19). When a woman seeks revenge, she smears her mystery with the grime of unforgiveness, and that is decidedly unattractive, not only to God, but to other people as well. Whether you realize it or not, those around you are watching, including the man in your life. They're observing how you act, how you talk, and how you respond in the face of opposition.

Scripture provides us with an alternative to revenge. "Instead, be kind to each other, tenderhearted, forgiving one another, just as God through Christ has forgiven you" (Ephesians 4:32). The Woman of Mystery seeks a spirit of forgiveness when someone has wronged her. Not only is she striving to trust God with her conflicts, but she is also creating a grace-filled environment around her. We cannot accept forgiveness from God for our mistakes and in turn not offer it to others for theirs. And so we must choose the difficult path of forgiveness and trust God to take care of righting the wrong for us.

When I was twelve years old, my dad left me. I suppose he

left my mom, but it sure felt like he left me. Over the next few years, I grew to hate him and his new wife. I became alienated and broken. I wanted my dad back but never got him. Then when I was eighteen, I had a revelation. He was only human and weak himself; it would be insanity for me to demand perfection from him. So I went to him to forgive him for what he had done in my life. He hadn't asked for forgiveness, and when I offered it, it seemed to make no impact. The response I wanted wasn't there. He acted like he'd always acted—distant and casual. But this time I didn't blame him. I accepted him and forgave him, and out of that came healing. Then, just a few years later, I got what I wanted. He apologized and asked for my forgiveness. He had found Christ and was a new creature, and our relationship was healed. But it all started with my willingness to let go of my right to harbor resentment. And that is really at the heart of forgiveness. We shouldn't be surprised when others sin; we all sin and fall short of the glory of God (see Romans 3:23). But the Woman of Mystery freely forgives others for their offenses against her. She isn't looking for retribution or revenge because she trusts God with all of that.

Her Essence Is Always Improving

The Woman of Mystery is always getting better. She is a better woman today than she was yesterday. And that is the beauty of her essence. When you desire to love and please God, you are continually becoming more and more like Jesus. The goal of the Woman of Mystery is never to stop growing but always to strive for more understanding and self-control. One of the best ways to grow is to make it your goal to study human nature—to read other people, understand their needs, tap into their fears and hopes. As you grow in knowledge and understanding of others, you will have more to offer in conversation and more compassion and empathy for those you talk to. The Woman of Mystery is a student of life, and because of that she is very interesting to be around. When you stop learning, you stop growing, and that kind of stagnancy squelches the deeper life we're called to (see Philippians 3:13-14). The Woman of Mystery is forever growing, forever learning, forever improving. I know it can be hard to find time to incorporate this into your already busy schedule, but there are ways you can spend time learning. Watch the news, watch the Discovery Channel, read biographies and blogs on interesting topics, join a group where you can learn something about a hobby or a ministry. Get involved in life; don't just let it come at you as it may. Be intentional about what you ingest mentally.

Of course, the best place to look to learn about human nature is God's Word itself. Those busy days when you feel like there's no way you can squeeze in time for the Bible are probably the days you need it most. A busy day is truly unmanageable without time devoted to studying the Bible to set your perspective in the right place. I know I have a tendency to covet sleep, because I get very little. When 6:30 a.m. rolls around and my daughter is ready to begin the day, I cover my head with my pillow and moan. I'm just not ready. So it seemed completely unimaginable to start waking up at 5:30 every morning to spend some time alone with God before Addy got up. But it was something I needed to do to work toward the degree of self-control I was looking for in my life. And so I started to rise at this unbearable hour, and after a while I noticed something: my usually tired body suddenly had energy. No longer was I dragging after lunch, but I had power to write, send e-mails, and work around the house while my daughter took her nap, rather than wanting to crawl up next to her and sleep as much as possible. Giving time to God in the form of Bible study and prayer has payoffs on so many levels. But one of the biggest is that it helps you to truly learn about the kind of woman God wants you to be, because God himself is the pattern we imitate. The more we seek him and find out about who he is, the more we learn about who we are and how to find joy and peace in every aspect of our lives.

Her Essence Rests

For many of us, busyness has strangled out any chance for this kind of mystery and attention to the deeper things. Our to-do lists color our views of life and the ways we treat those around us. I know that life can sometimes feel like a cross between a juggling act, a marathon, and firefighting. You are worn out. And no wonder—you do so much. Your life never truly slows down. But what if for a moment it could? What if you could say no to a few things and yes to even fewer? What if you never again had to say to your friends, "I'm too busy"? What if you never again had to tell your children, "Hurry up"? Sounds like an impossibility, but when a woman decides that busyness is taking away more than it's giving, she has the power to change not only her life but also the lives of those around her. And choosing to say no to something that someone else could do as well as you—or things you are doing out of obligation, not because they're things God has called you to—is a good place to start. If you are willing to stop hurrying and start living, you will find more depth and fullness in your relationship with God, in your relationships with the people in your life, and within your own soul. When you no longer say, "I don't have time for you," but suddenly decide, "These dishes can wait; how was your day?" you give your husband romantic energy. He suddenly feels loved and respected; he's stronger, more manly, and confident in your acceptance. It might be hard to put down the laptop or get off the phone, but in the end you have to ask yourself, *On my list of important things, where does this man sit? In the top three or on page three?* How you answer that is a big part of how much romance you can add to your life.

If you are single and this kind of relationship doesn't apply to you now, it doesn't mean you can't begin to prioritize relationships over tasks. You are training yourself to be the woman you want to be—whether you get married someday or not. So practice slowing down. Know when you need to say, "That project can wait till tomorrow. You're hurting—let's talk." You learn to make people and relationships more important than projects or promotions. This doesn't have to happen every time, but be open to ways you can love God and love others as yourself rather than achieving more or making more.

If you are willing to let God speak to you through his Word and his Spirit, you can begin to find the rest your heart craves. The demands on you may never cease, but it will be well with your soul. God never promised us rest from our trials: "Here on earth you will have many trials and sorrows. But take heart, because I have overcome the world" (John 16:33). But Jesus said that there can be rest in him: "Take my yoke upon you. Let me teach you, because I am humble and gentle at heart, and you will find rest for your souls. For my yoke is easy to bear, and the burden I give you is light" (Matthew 11:29-30).

Lifting the Veil

STRANGER PREP

Not too comfortable around strangers and people who serve you? Take some time to prepare before you go into a restaurant or another place where you're the customer. Be ready to look people in the eyes. Commit to remembering their names. Think of some good questions to ask people you meet to show you're truly interested in them. Kindness and humility aren't born; they're learned through patience and practice. So take lessons from kind people and come up with your own ways to give compliments or serve others.

BECOME A STUDENT

Part of being a Woman of Mystery is being teachable. Most of us stop reading for growth and learning after we're finished with school. But the more you learn, the more your depth as a woman can grow. So make a master list of titles you want to read and come up with a plan of attack so you can read more this year than last year. Find a mentor and meet with her weekly. Join a group that will help you grow in a particular area of need. Learn a new language. Get your brain moving.

DEVELOP HOPE

Get to work on developing your hope muscle. Make a list of at least ten things you can put your hope in. If you have trouble, look to God's Word and find his promises that give you hope. Keep this list close to you when feelings of hopelessness hit. Also create a hope hit list—things that destroy hope and need to be removed. For you it might be worrying or complaining. It could be living in fear or reliving the past. Whatever things trigger your bouts of hopelessness, write them down and then remind yourself to take those thoughts captive. Retrain your brain to think hopeful instead of hopeless thoughts.

her *Love*

I love that you get cold when it's 71 degrees out. I love that it takes you an hour and a half to order a sandwich. I love that you get a little crinkle above your nose when you're looking at me like I'm nuts. I love that after I spend the day with you, I can still smell your perfume on my clothes. And I love that you are the last person I want to talk to before I go to sleep at night.

• WHEN HARRY MET SALLY

There are only four questions of value in life. What is sacred? Of what is the spirit made? What is worth living for and what is worth dying for? The answer to each is the same. Only love.

• DON JUAN DEMARCO

Do I exist for my own personal happiness? No, my whole existence is devoted to her, even in spite of her. And by what right should I have dared to aspire to her love? What does it matter, so that it does not injure her happiness? My duty is to keep close to her steps, to surround her existence with mine, to serve her as a barrier against all dangers; to offer my head as a stepping-stone, to place myself unceasingly between her and all sorrows, without claiming reward, without expecting recompense. . . . Alas! If she only allow me to give my life to anticipating her every desire, all her caprices; if she but permit me to kiss with

The Difference between Love & Romance

Love and earthly romance often generate similar feelings. But they aren't mutually exclusive. Many a woman has experienced the sensation of romance and the feeling of love in the presence of a man who turned out to be anything but in love. Romance can be the ultimate expression of a man's love for a woman, but it might be nothing more than a kind gesture or an attempt toward conquest. Love can be expressed through romance, but romance doesn't require love. When something is romantic, it generates a feeling of euphoria. It is a natural high. Take away the soaring emotions and excitement, and you take away the romance. But love is not just a feeling. It can and often does feel like a natural high, but love doesn't always feel good. Christ's life is the best example of this. I am quite sure that the love that drove him to the Cross didn't always feel like a natural high but was exceedingly painful, both physically and emotionally. Love can best be understood as an action—not born of circumstances or feelings, but by a decision of the will. Romance, however, can often be confused with love because of the ability of both to create feelings of excitement and well-being. And that is often where women can get into trouble—considering romance a sure sign of love.

respect her adored footprints; if she but consent to lean upon me at times amidst the difficulties of life.

Victor Hugo penned these words as his heart welled up with love for his Woman of Mystery. To Hugo, her essence was his elixir. His heart was overflowing with love for the mystery of this woman. Wouldn't you love to have a man think so highly of you, to want you so much, to do whatever it took to protect you and adore you? I think this kind of love is something the heart of every woman craves. We desperately want to be wanted, even needed. We want romance, adoration, and attention. As little girls, we wanted this attention from our fathers. We danced with them, we imagined ourselves as their princesses, and we burrowed into their arms for protection and comfort. It is every woman's fantasy to be loved by her prince and every woman's dream to become his princess. Even for those of us who are pragmatic realists, there is still a part of our hearts that deep down yearns for a pure connection with a man—a man who finds us to be the most important person on earth.

The most universal of human desires is the longing to be loved. As human beings, we find that it occupies our hearts and our minds. When we fail to find love, we often languish in resentment and depression. And when we are rejected by love, we can find ourselves angry and bitter. Love is what we all crave more than anything else on earth; even the other things we seek all boil down to love. Attention, affirmation, success—all of it ultimately boils down to love. *Does someone love me? Does everyone love me?* When someone doesn't love us, it feels uncomfortable and injurious. Like the Father himself, we know instinctively that love is the greatest thing of all (see 1 Corinthians 13:13).

For the feminine heart, love means freedom to be who we were meant to be. It is the complete acceptance we crave, and because it fills a deep longing inside of us, we are certain it is precious. But by holding love in such high esteem, we often define it very rigidly— from our own limited perspectives. "If he loved me he would . . ." "If I were loved I would . . ." We often have romantic notions of what love really is. In fact, many times romance and love get confused in our hearts. We see or experience earthly romance, and to our hearts it is translated as love. We are certain that it is the ultimate expression of love.

God himself is curiously obsessed with love. The two greatest commandments given by God both involve this fascinating and desired verb: "Love the LORD your God with all your heart, all your soul, all your strength, and all your mind" and "Love your neighbor as yourself" (Luke 10:27). We are commanded not to seek love for ourselves but to give love to God and others. Perhaps it is because of our innate desire to be loved that God gave us this command. Knowing how much we would desire it, he commanded us to give love freely so that all might find the love they crave. God is always coming up with smart plans like that. Since God's Word doesn't command us to attain love but to give it, it is important in the search for mystery that we understand this fundamental spiritual component of love. Love is an action commanded by God, not just a feeling generated by romance.

Romance, rather, can stem from a person's desire to express the love that one has for another. For a woman, romance is more often received than given, and that is simply because a man, for the most part, isn't looking for romance to feel love. He is giving it as an expression of his love or because he has been told that it is required of him. You rarely hear a man complaining that there isn't enough romance in the relationship or begging to go to the latest romantic comedy. By nature, the typical man isn't prone to craving romance, while the typical woman is. Most men go to romantic movies because the women they love want to go. Romance and all the trappings of it are primarily designed to please the heart of a woman. Though there may be the occasional man who craves red roses and a room filled with candles, for the most part he craves what comes as a result of those things, not those things themselves.

When a man loves a woman, he tells her so with romantic gestures. And her heart gets it. There aren't many women who can feel truly loved when there is a total lack of romance. And that is because we tend to believe that if a man truly loves a woman, it will generate such an emotion in him that he can't help but express it in the form of romance. There is some truth to that notion. When a man loves a woman, truly loves her, he can't contain himself—he must give her what she desires, or his love is wasted by keeping it to himself. He wants to go outside of himself and shower his love on her. When a man simply feels affection for a woman or a practical need for her, he shows her respect and treats her with kindness, but he doesn't take the risk of romance. For the most part, romance is how a woman first knows that a man is interested in her. It is his way of saying "I love you" or "I might love you" without using any words. And innately women know that.

Her Love Lets Him Lead

Romance is organic. It isn't easily managed or fabricated. But manufactured romance tells us it's possible if only we create the right setting, wear the right clothes, play the right music, or look just the right way. Though it's true that setting can amplify romance, real earthly romance isn't as easy as inviting it over and asking it to get to work. It requires time. It requires a true and abiding focus. Demanding that love hurry up or that romance make its move is like deciding that you need to drop twenty pounds and telling God to make it happen by morning. There are no shortcuts to romantic love. Becoming demanding or impatient for love will never till the soil of romance. So when a single woman is anxious to marry and makes that angst known to the man she's interested in, the recipe is disaster. Urgency is never mysterious. When she demonstrates a sense of fear about being alone or restlessness with being single, she removes the dim lighting of romance and turns on the harsh lights of desperation—the kind that cause a man to put one hand to his eyes to stop the blinding glare and the other up to hail a taxi. When a woman makes demands or pushes the natural order of things, she might feel like she's taking charge and using her strength to get where she wants to go. But that's like ripping the cocoon off of the caterpillar because you can't wait to set the butterfly free. When you open up a cocoon prematurely, you end up with an underdeveloped butterfly that will never fly, let alone survive. Simply put, impatience and love don't go together (see 1 Corinthians 13:4). The grand secret to finding romance is not to demand it or to rush it, but to be patient and let it unfold at just the right time.

I've had some firsthand experience with learning patience. I didn't meet the man of my dreams until I was thirty-six years old. Looking back, I know now that the timing was just right. Any earlier and neither of us would have been prepared for the life and ministry God had planned for us.

If you are single, and if you are willing to let love do its work and let God be God, then teach yourself these tips: don't talk to him first, don't initiate phone calls, don't ask him out, don't pay for him, don't tell him what to do, and don't push yourself into his life. Because any attempt to do these things reveals a heart of desperation. Pushing him to like you or to do things with you is just that: it is pushing, and pushing is the opposite of the direction you wish he would go. It is no secret that something that is hard to get is more valuable than something that requires little or no effort. Men are competitive by nature: they conquer, they battle, and they achieve. And when we allow our desires for control to overwhelm or overshadow those tendencies in a man, we remove the mystery. And for a man, not only is mystery alluring, but so is pursuit. If a man is interested, he will pursue you; if not, then he won't. Shyness might slow him down, but when a man is interested, nothing gets in his way. I would love to tell you to decide what you want and go after it. But I know from countless experiences, as well as study, that the "Just Do It" concept works well for material desires, dreams, and sneakers, but not so well when it involves another human being with hopes, dreams, and thoughts of his own. Bullying or managing love into existence is living outside of the mystery, and though it might work for a season, it will not generate the true romance that your heart so deeply craves.

I once met a woman who asked a guy out, took him on a date, and paid. They hit it off and started to date. Months later she complained to me that he never planned anything or did anything romantic for her. She was shocked when she realized that she had never given him a need to do any of those things since she did them all. She had trained him that she would plan and pay, so why would things change now? Everything was going so well for him. We set a pattern early on with a man when we force romance and even a relationship. But a patient expectation and a willingness to be overlooked if he's just not that into her gives a woman an air of mystery that will one day allure just the right man.

In a marriage relationship, romance cannot be rushed or demanded either. Surely, he is yours, and he should express his love for you. But do you really want romance only because you demanded it or orchestrated it and he just showed up for it? There can be moments of elation in those situations, but they are fleeting, and then resentment often follows. Unfortunately, there is no biblical mandate for a man to romance his wife. Oh, that there were! I would post it on the bathroom mirror and on the fridge door. Earthly romance is beautiful, but not essential, to the life of a woman. When we demand romance and tell ourselves that we are incomplete without it, we place our hope and salvation in something that was never intended to be either. It is an interesting twist of life, however, that when we stop pursuing our "rights" so relentlessly, often that very thing soon presents itself to us in the most mysterious ways. Though my desire is that all of us will find more romance than we can handle, I also pray that if we don't, we will find all the hope and salvation we need in the God who freely offers both.

Her Love Understands Him

In the pursuit of mystery and romantic love, it is important for both single and married women to understand the minds of men. Men are a great deal different from women. They have different ideas, different desires, and different ways of thinking. And perhaps most significantly, different ways of experiencing love. In his book *His Needs, Her Needs*, author Willard F. Harley Jr. reveals some basic differences between the ways men and women interpret love. Here is a list of the top five needs, or as I prefer to say, wants, that men and women are looking for in a marriage. Most men place their desires in this order: sexual fulfillment, recreational companionship, an attractive wife, domestic support, and admiration. In contrast, most women rank their needs for feeling loved in this order: affection, conversation, honesty and openness, financial support, and family commitment. Most of us find it easy, and almost natural, to offer the kind of love to others that we ourselves desire. As women, we might offer affection, conversation, honesty, and openness, and determine that is true love. We assume we're giving a man all he needs. But when we

I do not like to think of you as needing to have 'things' pleasant around you when you have God within you. Surely He is enough to content any soul. If He is not enough here, how will it be in the future life when we have only Him Himself?

– Hannah Whitall Smith

look at this list, it's obvious how different a man's desires are. Love thrives not when we give what we need but when we give what the person we love needs. When the Golden Rule says we're to do to others as we'd want them to do to us (see Luke 6:31), it doesn't mean we're to give others the exact things *we* desire. If you've ever given a gift to a friend who has entirely different tastes from you, then you understand that doing to others as you would have them do unto you is about choosing to give a friend what he or she desires just as you would want to have your desires met and cared for.

I once had a friend who got this concept completely wrong. She was a perky Martha Stewart type: Good around the home, always entertaining, very busy in the kitchen. Super charming, but completely different from me. I'm a bit more of a bohemian, if you will. I'm more of a bowl of spaghetti and garlic bread type of entertainer. I don't do fancy dinner parties or sculpt fruit bowls out of real fruit. So when she gave me a set of cocktail forks for my birthday, I had to laugh. She gave me, more than likely, exactly what she wanted. Obviously cocktail forks aren't going to make or break a relationship, but the question is out there: When you attempt to express love, are you giving others what *you* deeply desire? Or are you able to show love in a way that speaks to the other person? Are you able to live outside of yourself?

Her Love Honors Him

God's Word contains much of the recipe for romance. And it all centers around how we love. We are called to "love each other with genuine affection, and take delight in honoring each other" (Romans 12:10). Love by its very nature is extravagant in honoring the object of its affection. It holds the one it loves in high regard and respect. And the interesting truth is that honor comes before romance, not the other way around. It might be just a coincidence, but in most wedding vows, you hear first of love, then honor, and finally cherishing. A groom loves, honors, and respects his bride, so he finds ways to express that in romantic moments that show how cherished she is. She honors and respects him, and that drives him to generate romantic opportunities. More than likely, a woman who disrespects a man upon first meeting him isn't going to get much romance out of him. For the married or committed woman, honor is the fuel that sends your husband's mind soaring as he conceives new and ingenious ways to love you. Honor can be a doorway to romance for you. When you set your mind on honoring the man you love, you set your mind not only on his virtues but also on the virtues of the hands that created him. Perhaps that's a part of what God had in mind when he asked a woman to honor her man (see Ephesians 5:33). The truth is that men are exhilarated by honor. They become emboldened and brave in the face of it. When a man feels honored, when he is shown how important he is to the very life of the woman he loves, he gains strength and hope. A man who feels little honor or respect from his woman is often weak, deflated, or even defeated. And he most often lacks any energy or drive to create romantic moments.

Your man may have failed to honor you. He may have lost the fire that initially drove him to romantic expressions of love. He might be distracted or even at odds with you, but that doesn't make his existence and his manliness any less of a miracle. When romance is dead, a woman has three options: She can give up and take whatever limited affection she can get. Or she can fight for what she desires and make demands of and complaints to her man. Or she can step out in faith and keep loving him and honoring him, whether it seems like he deserves it or not. She can choose to believe that if she obeys God's Word and loves based not on what a man does but on who he is, she will ultimately find for herself a romance that has less to do with what she's getting and more to do with what she is giving. When a man doesn't provide the romance a woman needs, it can be very easy for her emotions and passionate affections to retaliate by responding to him with the same paltry measure. "I will only honor him as much as he honors me." "I won't respect him until he starts respecting me." But while that might sound sensible on a practical level, it makes no sense spiritually. And it only leaves us bitter and desperate for relief. I know this because I've been there.

I adore romance. I want to be twirled around the dance floor and dipped till dawn. I want to be showered with affection and covered with kisses. I want love to express itself in the shape of genuine romance. But life can sometimes get in the way of those kinds of plans. I remember a season in my marriage when romance was a distant memory to my heart, and I was lamenting the fact that the fire was gone from my previously steamy relationship. I considered how I might get it back. I thought of ways to ask my husband why it was missing, demand it, arrange for it. And then, in a moment of revelation, I found myself confronted with the fact that this wasn't just about him. I, too, had lost the spark of honor and awe in our relationship. And so I did the only thing I knew to do. I opened up my computer and began to write. I wrote these words: "I love Michael because . . ." and then I let my fingers tap away. I thought of everything amazing about him. I considered all his

> *A woman who gives admiration gets love.*

strengths and laid them all out on the screen. Then I determined to read this list every day. And each day my spark got bigger. But I didn't stop there—I also started to consider God's handiwork. I studied the way a man is wired. I read books about how he thinks, why he thinks, and what I should think. I read things that led me to admire my husband's manliness and all that it entails. And I learned to admire men in general and my husband in particular for the unique creation he is. For the first time, I looked at manhood from God's point of view. And burning in the center of my heart, I found more romance than I ever thought possible.

My life hadn't changed; my husband hadn't changed. But my romance had. Suddenly I looked at Michael differently. I thought more positive thoughts than negative ones. I saw in his long hours of work his beautiful drive to provide for his family. And I saw his criticism of my spending sprees not as a criticism of me but of my sin in letting myself go in an area that I'm struggling to control. And I admired him for being man enough to stand up to me and for being strong enough to hold this driven woman accountable in ways no man had had the fortitude to do before. I found joy in the fact that this man was more man than I. And I loved him for it.

Romance isn't only in the hands of the man who offers it. It is in your hands as well, and a large part of it has to do with your choice to honor the person God has gifted you with. When you can respect him for who he is, you are honoring not only him but also the God who imagined him and created him and sent him to you in the first place.

Her Love Admires Him

One of the biggest needs of a man is his need to be admired.

From what my husband and other men tell me, admiration feels to a man the way romance feels to a woman. It builds his confidence and sends his mind racing toward ideas of eternal bliss and a happy life with the woman who admires him. It gives him power and strength. It makes his world a bit brighter and his challenges a bit easier. Admiration is a gift of pure love to a man, with the added benefit of growing romance in the heart of a woman. So how can you begin cultivating an attitude of admiration? This proverb gives us a starting point: "For as he thinketh in his heart, so is he" (Proverbs 23:7, KJV). Your thoughts cannot fail to produce emotions in your heart. If you think negative thoughts, you will grow negative emotions. Think positive thoughts, and you will find yourself with positive emotions. It's not just a psychological phenomenon but a biblical principle. Watch it unfold in these verses: "Whatsoever things are true, whatsoever things are honest, whatsoever things are just, whatsoever things are pure, whatsoever things are lovely, whatsoever things are of good report; if there be any virtue, and if there be any praise, think on these things. Those things, which ye have both learned, and received, and heard, and seen in me, do: and the God of peace shall be with you" (Philippians 4:8-9, KJV). Did you catch that? God has asked us to focus on things that are good and praiseworthy, things that are lovely and of good report, and this includes the things that are good about the men in our lives. And as an added bonus, the more you concentrate on a man's good attributes, the more earthly romance you will begin to feel.

It is truly a thing of mystery to a man when a woman admires him. Deep down, a man, just like a woman, feels inadequate. He wonders who could love him and what within him is noble or noteworthy. And when a man finds a woman who admires his qualities, he finds himself enamored with her affection and the attention she pays to who he is on the inside and out.

You know how it feels when a man finds you beautiful? When he admires your lips, your hair, your skin? You know how you feel when he compliments the beauty of your personality, your character, your faith? It makes you feel more complete, more loved, and more beautiful with each word. A man is not so different. He might not say it, but he loves it when you admire all that is masculine in him. His strength, his mind, his body, his muscles, his success, his integrity. Your admiration means the world to the man who loves you, so lavish it on him with all the love you can muster. If you find it hard to generate admiration, here are some things to consider about your man: his strength, his body, his mental toughness, his chivalry, his skills and talents, his ability to lead, his willingness to take risks, his masculinity, his achievements and successes, his emotional strength when faced with difficult circumstances, his backbone, his tendency to get over hurts and anger easily, his drive to provide, and his ability to think clearly and avoid overanalyzing everything.

My husband is a genius—his IQ is off the charts—and I appreciate that about him. But there are times when he starts telling me about something technological, mechanical, or political that is completely out of my realm of comprehension. And I have no idea why he is choosing to share it with me. I remember several years ago when he taught himself a new computer program that allowed him to create amazing Web sites (and in doing so, save us thousands of dollars), and he was so excited that he told me all the little details of the program and what it could do for us and our business. The truth was, I didn't understand what he was talking about, nor did I really care about all of it. But I knew it meant a lot to him and he really wanted to share his success at mastering this new thing with me. So I listened, and although I didn't get most of it, I heard him out. He was happy, and because of that, so was I. Sometimes men will talk to you about things that are out of your realm of interest or expertise, just to get your admiration. How else could you admire him if you didn't know the lengths to which he has gone to achieve something? To love a man the way he needs to be loved is to listen to him intently, even if what he's saying isn't particularly interesting or applicable to you. When you truly listen to the man in your life with the desire to find out more about him, to admire him, you give that man the gift of love, and you seed the ground for the growth of romance.

Her Love Chooses to Need Him

There is a fine line that mystery walks between independence and interdependence. If a woman is lacking independence, she comes across to a man as desperate and needy. If mystery is going to do its work, a woman must be independent enough not to put all her hopes on the shoulders of a man. This is something I learned before I got married as I made a life for myself without a man by my side. I had a wonderful home on a golf course. I loved my career, my car, my friends. I traveled. I was successful by anyone's terms. And I believe that independence was often what drew men to me. I know that Michael certainly appreciated it. And in it he found a mystery waiting to be cracked. Rather than waiting at home for a man to complete me, I was living life to the fullest. I didn't need a man to make me happy, though I desired one, and I didn't live and die by the success or failure of love. And that is very attractive to a man. So independence, the ability to find joy with or without a man, is a very mysterious and alluring quality.

But for now let's talk about the flip side of the topic: what if a woman is *too* independent? A man could think she has her life all planned out and there is no room left for him. How can a woman show herself willing and able to become appropriately interdependent with a man? I knew of a dear and beautiful man named Ferg, who loved and devoted his life to his wife, Lesla, for sixty-five years. He raised two children with her, provided for her, and saw their children grow, flourish, and succeed as adults. As this man and his wife got older, she started needing him more and more. Eventually she could no longer walk or care for herself. And so he did everything for her. He loved her so much that taking care of her was his joy. But at the age of eighty-nine, when her body couldn't go on any longer, she left him. He sat down in a chair in their living room and said, "I've served my purpose. Now it's time for me to die." And one week later, he went to join his wife in glory. We all grieved that day, but we also rejoiced as Ferg and Lesla were together again for eternity. Ferg, like most men, found his life, his purpose, in being needed. When he was no longer needed and had done what he believed he was put on earth to do, he was ready to go.

In order to feel loved, a man must feel needed. Need says to a man's soul that he has a purpose. But needing a man must be done not out of desperation but out of a true admiration for his strengths and gratitude for his help. When I got married, I was a very independent woman, and I didn't need Michael to survive. But I *chose* to need him and become interdependent with him. In our relationship, we have learned to work together by doing things that we are each good at. The net result is that both of us get to be relieved and supported by one another.

Men and women both need to be needed in a romantic relationship, but this need expresses itself in different ways. For the most part, the difference is revealed in the expression of romance. A woman desires to be needed for a man's very life. She wants her presence to at least symbolically be his reason for living. She wants him to find he needs her to be complete, to find joy. She wants to be needed as a person who offers him what no one else ever has or ever will. A man has a slightly different take on need. He wants to be needed but for much more tangible purposes. He wants to be needed to provide things, to lift things, to fight off things. He wants to be her protector, her knight in shining armor who rescues her from the dragon's clutches. He doesn't want to be needed to be the breath in her lungs or the reason she's alive. That all can seem a bit impractical and overstated to the typical man. If we don't understand this fundamental difference, it can get us into trouble. A single woman who lets a man know that he is her everything, that she can't live without him, and in fact that she would surely die if he left, runs the risk of shattering the romance—and possibly even the relationship—with her overdependence. She might interpret his backing off as a fear of commitment, but it might be more a fear of having to be her everything. When a woman can learn to need a man only in ways he is designed to be needed, she can greatly reduce his fear of being smothered by her love.

So what are some ways a man *does* need to be needed? Let him get the door for you. Even though you've opened the door a thousand times before, let him do you the honor, and let him feel like

her Love

a man. When you are carrying a heavy box or something cumbersome, ask him to help you. Expressing a need for him and his masculine strength can be an act of love. Or ask him to open the pickle jar. Let him pick you up in his car, walk you to the door, and pull out your chair for you. Let him do the manly things around the house without redoing them after he's potentially botched them. Anything that involves a hammer, a drill, or any other manly tool is usually best left to him. Not that you can't do it. Goodness knows, when I bought my 1940s cottage as a single woman, I did my fair share of home improvements. I had all the tools needed to repair anything from a hole in the wall to a broken toilet. But after I got married, I found out that my husband took great joy in doing all the "tool stuff" for me. And when I bypassed him and just did it myself so I could get it done, he felt useless. "What do you need me for if you can drill your own holes and pound your own nails?" he once said. Not that he believes that's all he's good for, but it gives him purpose and makes him feel important in our relationship. If you are constantly trying to do it all yourself, you are communicating to him that what you value most is practicality. And romance is anything but practical.

Her Love Accepts Him

At the heart of love is the desire to be accepted. Though the world turns on you, though your boss dismisses you, though your parents fail you, the man who truly loves you will always take you as you are. No matter how your face sags or your hair grays, he will accept you. Acceptance is a generous part of romance. Acceptance from a man comes in the form of adoration. His adoration tells your heart that he accepts every part of you, and you are lifted up by his love. There is something so freeing—and so reflective of God's unconditional love—when you experience this kind of acceptance, when someone sees your strengths and your weaknesses and your quirks and still loves you. And as much as you crave this kind of acceptance, a man also needs it from you. You are quite possibly the only person who will ever accept him completely. And when you fail to accept him, he is crushed.

When a woman starts to date a man, she must consider this crucial fact: he is who he is. Any notion in the back of her mind that she will change him or fix him or make him better for her is wasted thought. When a man falls in love with you, you want him to love you for who you are, not who he imagines you could be. How tragic if he felt you had potential but needed some tweaking before he could love you. No, romance says, "I accept you just how you are." Sure, there are stains on all of us, some areas we could all work on, sins we shouldn't allow into our lives. But when it comes to the core of who you are, you want him to accept you. And your role is to do the same for him. Asking a man to change—or demanding it—is the killer of acceptance. And it can easily leave him uninspired and broken.

If you want your man to change, consider asking yourself two questions. The first one is, *Why do I want to change him? Is it to make my life better?* If the answer is yes, then it's time to take stock of what your happiness and sense of security are based on. Is your life really dependent on what this man says and does? Or is it based on your relationship with God? Any notion that a man is responsible for your happiness is not only a lie but also a real strain on your relationship. That kind of pressure puts too much onto the shoulders of a man, and he will end up resenting it. He wasn't made to be your sole source of happiness. So if that's your reason for wanting him to change, it's not a fair expectation. Indeed, a man wasn't made to be the source of true romance, but rather one of many gifts from a God who created and sustains the romance in all areas of life.

The second question to ask yourself with regard to changing your man is, *Am I seeking change in order to make him a better man?* That may sound good, but is that really your responsibility? Or is it God's? A woman can't allow a false sense of nobility to be the reason she rejects her man and demands a makeover of his life. Love demands that she accept him, flaws and all, just as she hopes he accepts her. As believers, we must know that it isn't a woman who changes a man, but God. Your greatest ally and strength is God himself, not your powers of persuasion. I have found time and again that when there is an area in Michael's life where I feel he is missing it spiritually, I pray and I pray, and I wait for God to reveal the same thing to him. If you want your man to change, talk to God about it—daily!

It is often said that a man romances a woman until he catches her, and then he goes back to his masculine, unromantic ways. And that is often the case. When we marry, many women have this fantastical idea that life will forever be filled with romantic highs. But from a man's perspective, he sees it as impractical to keep up the chase after he's caught the one he was pursuing. Of course, ideally, the man would continue to do his part to romance his wife. But if he doesn't, it's not beneficial to you or him or anyone else to obsess over his failure to do so. It will just make you bitter and depressed. It won't bring you any closer to getting what you want, and in fact, it will most likely drive you further from it. The only thing we truly have control of in this life is ourselves—our thoughts and our actions. We cannot, no matter how much elbow grease we put in, make other people do what we want them to do as long as they don't want to do it. So that leaves us with one option: to work on what we can—ourselves.

When another person sins or even just disappoints you, it is never an excuse for your sin. Even if his sin is ugly and terrible or if he has let you down in a big way, it is never a free pass to sin in return. My favorite verse to that effect is 1 Peter 2:23: "[Jesus] did not retaliate when he was insulted, nor threaten revenge when he suffered. He left his case in the hands of God, who always judges fairly." I love the honor and strength of Christ. He certainly could have brought about some mighty retribution. But his love for us was too powerful. And so he left us that moment as an example. No matter how sad our romantic lives are, no matter how much men hurt us when they reject us, pass us by, or ignore us, we cannot and will not be swayed from the course of faith. For we entrust our lives, even the unfair and difficult parts, to him who holds the world in his hands. And we know, after all, that his love is the only love that will truly sustain us. In our pursuit of romance, it is crucial that we find true romance first at the feet of the Savior and then allow it to unfold with the man who loves us. The Woman of Mystery understands that any earthly relationship is a supplemental relationship to the most important and central of all relationships: the one with the God who will "rejoice over you with singing" (Zephaniah 3:17, NIV). Choose to love the way God loves, and leave the results to him. "Live a life filled with love, following the example of Christ. He loved us and offered himself as a sacrifice for us, a pleasing aroma to God" (Ephesians 5:2).

Lifting the Veil

MAKE A LIST

If you have a man, make a list of all the good things about him. Read it each morning, and comment on those good qualities throughout the day, especially in front of others. If you don't have a man, make a list of the good things about your life. Practice contentment by reading your list every day and thanking God for all the good things in your life.

INDEPENDENT THINKING?

Make three columns: *independent*, *interdependent*, and *dependent*. In the first column, write things you don't need a man for. In the middle column, write things you *can* do but would rather depend on him for. Lastly, list things you can't (or won't) do yourself. Include specific feelings, activities, projects around the house, acts of chivalry, etc. Could anything on your independent list be taking away from his sense of providing? Are things on the interdependent and dependent lists making you too clingy? Do your lists need any rearranging?

LORD, PLEASE CHANGE HIM

If you are married and something in your husband's life is negatively impacting him or the family, pray about his problems and read the Bible to confirm that this is something God wants to change. As an ambassador of your family, confess his sin as your sin, remembering the two of you are one (see Joshua 24:15). Then ask God to reveal truth to your husband. Pray as long and as often as possible. If what you are up against is dangerous to your husband or your family, you may also need to talk with your husband and a counselor or pastor. If you aren't married and desire a man, seek God and know yourself to determine if you were made for a relationship with just God or with a man as well, and then ask for it. Trust that God has a man for you, and then pray for him.

her Lips

I love him and I don't care what you think. I love him for the man
he wants to be, and I love him for the man that he almost is.
• JERRY MAGUIRE

In her love I am the hero, the king, the poet. Without her love, I am
nothing at all, not even truly alive.
• UNKNOWN

I can remember some three-hour marathons on the phone with
Michael when he lived on the West Coast and I lived in the
South. We would get on the phone at 10:00 p.m. and not hang
up till 1:00 or 2:00 in the morning. It was sheer ecstasy. He was
so witty and so quick. He flirted well, telling me what he liked
about me in cute ways, like comparing me to his favorite cereal
and then asking me to compare him to mine. I loved his mind and
his verbal adoration. For those few hours I felt truly special and
accepted, and it was incredible. We connected in ways that only
words can connect two people. Yes, I am pretty sure that talking
is an aphrodisiac to a woman in love. The more you talk with the

man you're interested in, the more you want him. The more you want him, the more you fall for him. Talking has got to be one of the biggest turn-ons for the smitten woman.

I think that quite possibly words are the most amazing thing in the world. With words I share love with my family and friends. With words I make myself known and get to know others. So how fitting that God would refer to Jesus as the Word (see John 1:1). Jesus was the Word God used to make himself known to us. It is through the Word and the Word alone that we are allowed to know the Father. "My Father has entrusted everything to me. No one truly knows the Son except the Father, and no one truly knows the Father except the Son and those to whom the Son chooses to reveal him" (Matthew 11:27).

Jesus' life on earth was an expression of God's love for us. His Word spoke to us and shared love and life with us, just as our words connect us to those we love.

Words are often the vehicle of love and hope. Designed to communicate with our very souls, words are a delicious delicacy that I often cannot seem to get enough of. When it comes to relationships, the more words I share with a person, the more connected I feel to him or her.

Have you found an outlet for your soul's emotions? Have you found an ear that will take the time to truly get to know you—someone who yearns to experience every moment of your life with you? And have you found the ability to do the same for someone else? If so, then you have found an amazing thing. Unfortunately, for most men talking is not a passion. Maybe that's why songwriters and poets (and maybe even male leads in romantic movies) instill such romance in the heart of a woman—because they seem

her Lips

to share our natural desire to communicate words with another's heart. But since most of us don't live with Shakespeare or John Mayer, we need to develop healthy expectations of what communication will look like in our relationships.

Talking can be a powerful tool in the hand of a man who wants to win the heart of a woman. And it can also be an element of mystery in the hands of a smart woman. Knowing your audience is always key when it comes to drawing people into your story. If you want to create a successful story, you need to know the heart of the one you are inviting to experience it with you. Every word a woman chooses to say to a man has the potential to draw him to seek more, to dive deeper, and to go further than he's ever gone before. Understanding a man and his capacity for the spoken word (and his limits) is of great value to a woman who wishes to captivate the heart of a man.

> In the beginning the Word already existed.
> The Word was with God,
> and the Word was God.
> He existed in the beginning with God.
> God created everything through him,
> and nothing was created except through him.
> The Word gave life to everything that was created,
> and his life brought light to everyone.
> The light shines in the darkness,
> and the darkness can never extinguish it.
>
> JOHN 1:1-5

Her Words Are Measured

Just as we all need water to live, everyone needs words in order to connect. But too much water and the thirsty man will drown in the very element that he requires. The ancient proverb goes, "Too much talk leads to sin" (Proverbs 10:19). Mystery requires that a woman serve a man just enough water to quench but not enough to drown his love. The right words spoken at the right time are pure perfection. "Everyone enjoys a fitting reply; it is wonderful to say the right thing at the right time!" (Proverbs 15:23). But part of saying the right thing at the right time is managing your word count. By holding back enough to entice a man to take the next step, you create mystery, and he wants more.

At their core, men are conquerors; they love the adventure of the unknown. They crave danger, risk, and challenge. When a woman gives a man just enough information to send him on a mysterious adventure, his heart quickens. He becomes intrigued by her elusiveness. Many times, a single woman, in an attempt to be known, can make the mistake of saying too much too soon. She feels compelled to tell a man everything about her, everything that has happened to her, everything she feels, and everything she desires. These are parts of her that she wants validated—and rightly so—but not with any man who shows an interest in her. While that might feel good to her feminine heart temporarily, it leaves her emotionally exposed and vulnerable to men who haven't proved themselves worthy of such valuable parts of her. And it does one major thing to the man who sits across from her: it removes all the mystery.

The excitement that comes with the early stages of romance is most often found in the unknown. Will he like me? Will he get me? Will he kiss me? Everything we wonder about is what sends tingles up our spines. In the same way, what first draws a man to a woman is the possibility. The possibility that she is the one, the possibility that she might reject him but that it is well worth the risk. A woman needs to be wise in how much of herself she exposes to a man—and how quickly she does it. Romance requires a bit of reservation.

And so a woman holds the power of nurturing or squelching romance with the use of her lips. Will she choose to slow the pace and reveal just what is needed, or will she forgo the chance for romance in the hope that putting all the information out there will draw him to her? It's a gamble, but one that is certainly worth weighing wisely.

And there's a deeper purpose for the way we use our words. God, as the author of true romance, makes a clear connection between wisdom and keeping our words in check. "There is more hope for a fool than for someone who speaks without thinking" (Proverbs 29:20). And "too many words make you a fool" (Ecclesiastes 5:3). Too much information is too much for a reason. The key to eliciting an aura of mystery and romance is to live as the creator of true romance lived. Christ's very nature drew even the coldest heart to his side. The tax collectors, the harlots, the social outcasts—they all wanted more of what they were hearing and seeing in Jesus.

After a woman gets married and shares her life and heart with a man, he comes to know all her ins and outs. He finds out things others will never know about her, and he loves her even in spite of them, or maybe even because of them. But as time wears on and two people have the comfort of familiarity, romance can wane. This is normal, since true love plus time equals comfort and security. And this is a relaxing, safe, and restoring place to be, a place where you can be yourself, warts and all. So it's not all bad that romance fades over time. Can you imagine living in the high of early romantic love your entire life? I know for me three things would happen: I would never eat and never sleep, and work would be out of the question, because I would be too focused on the one I love. My thoughts would always return to his face, his hands, his mouth. I wouldn't be able to pay the bills or listen to a friend. I'd be a romantic wreck. And I suppose we experience something similar in our love relationship with the Savior. In the beginning we are high on the experience, and everyone else needs to hear about it. We are zealous and boisterous. We think we know it all and others need our help. We are crazy in love. But over time we mellow; we become comfortable in love. And some might say we accomplish more with this wisdom, though we do so quietly. Yes, romance must take a break. It can't be all romance all the time.

But at the same time, we don't want to let the romance fizzle out of our lives altogether. Obviously this requires the attention and commitment of both parties, but there's a lot you can do to keep a healthy amount of mystery in your relationship. One of the most significant ways you can do this is by checking your words.

While talking a lot may not only be enjoyable for you but also feel like a real need, you have to consider the hearer of the words. Is the other person encouraged and built up by your words, or is he drained by them? You are smart enough to know the difference. So use your intuition and your self-awareness and check yourself to see if you are talking with your man too much or just the right amount. In order to keep the mystery alive in your relationship, it is important to remember the principle that too much is too much. And consider allowing your man to be a man of few words—few words spoken and few words heard, if that is how he is wired.

How to Measure

Okay, so fewer words means more mystery, but if you're like me, you're asking, "How do I do that?" I am the kind of person who feels that if I can't talk with someone about what I've done, then it's like I haven't fully done it. The sad moments find release in the sharing, and the good moments find extended glory in the conversation about them. And so I hanker to talk about every moment of my day with my husband. But I have realized that hearing about my every moment, every complaint, every test is too much for his already full mind to handle.

I personally believe that my husband talks more than I do. He loves to talk—it's no secret. Yet he will still say that I am the big talker in the family. While I don't believe that is true in comparison, I think that probably demonstrates his desire to sometimes have silence be okay and to not have to be privy to all the workings of my daily life. And since I love him, I made a change and started spending more of my words on the women around me, who also have high word counts. I'd call my mom to tell her about my day or chat with a friend over lunch. And suddenly I had an outlet for all those things that screamed to be said, and when I was with Michael I could focus on the most important things we needed to communicate about. Keeping the mystery alive by not talking too much doesn't mean shutting up completely or avoiding talking about yourself, but it is a call to take turns, to make sure you're not monopolizing the conversation, to be willing to give and to take.

Communication is like a dance where you step forward and backward in unison—as ready to share as you are to listen. And it requires restraint in the area of dumping. If your motive is to be known and only to be known, then dumping might be your default mode. But if your motive is not only to be known but also to know, then you are able to begin the adventure of true mutual sharing.

Consider the words of Eugene Peterson in his paraphrase of the Bible's love chapter: "Love cares more for others than for self . . .

isn't always 'me first'" (1 Corinthians 13:4-7, *The Message*). Asking a man to suck it up so you can fulfill your word quota doesn't speak of mystery but of selfishness. And as followers of Christ, we have the privilege of going to God not only as our Savior but also as our Counselor (see Isaiah 9:6). When we share our hearts, our failures, and our trials with God, we free men from the expectation that they should carry all our thoughts on their shoulders.

Her Words Are Kind

Sometimes we reject the effort of speaking kindly because we feel it's a threat to our personalities or our freedom to express ourselves or our right to be whoever we want to be whenever we want to be. "I'm assertive—that's how I am. Deal with it." "I'm outgoing. I'm not flirting with that other man; I'm just being social." And we sacrifice kindness on the altar of individuality, neglecting to consider what our character weaknesses and even our strengths can do to those around us. The woman who understands mystery knows that everything is permissible but not everything is beneficial (see 1 Corinthians 6:12, NIV). And that means we need to consider the effects of who we are, who we are proud of being, on the people in our lives—friends, family members, and the men we love. Kindness says, "It's not only the sin in my life that must be denied, but at times even the good parts of me that must be sacrificed as well." Denying yourself something that in and of itself isn't sinful is an exercise in self-control and love. The apostle Paul lived this principle to his core: "I, too, try to please everyone in everything I do. I don't just do what is best for me; I do what is best for others so that many may be saved. And you should imitate me, just as I imitate Christ" (1 Corinthians 10:33–11:1). Just as

Christ humbled himself to the point of death for sins that were not even his own, so the woman steeped in mystery will learn to love from a position of humility and kindness rather than pride and self-actualization.

I'm the queen of inserting my foot into my mouth. I've been known to be very opinionated and have a fiery personality. Early in my career, I was often called on by ministry leaders, authors, and publishers to help guide people's writing careers. I was asked to give feedback on content and design and help people become better at what they did. It was pretty important for me to make my clients happy if I wanted to be paid, but I often found myself just saying whatever I was thinking. So when one particular leader asked me what my conclusion was about his books, I said, "You need to stop writing. You are killing too many trees!" I didn't exactly deliver the hard news in the best way, and needless to say, I didn't continue to consult him in his ministry.

In the past I have often opted to let it all hang out, no matter what casualties it caused around me. This was all part of the tragic worldview of "keeping it real." And though I often got my way with that method, I have since found that there's a better way. Learning to manage my words and edit what I say before I say it has been a grand coup for me and for those I love. It has taken years of intentionality, but I can tell you for certain that it was worth every effort.

Her Words Encourage

One of the easiest ways for a man to lose sight of the mystery is to listen to a woman speak poorly of others (see James 1:26). Most of the time when a man hears gossip, he shakes his head and walks away, figuratively or literally. Because to him, gossip has refrains of envy, selfishness, and pettiness. Manly men are not prone to gossip, nor do they understand how it can satisfy a woman's soul. They are simply not impressed by a woman who condemns or smears the lives of those she is called to love. I believe that our feminine addiction to gossip stems from a partially noble place inside our hearts—that place that yearns to be a part of the whole, to be connected to others, and to understand who they are. But when it gets twisted, that part of us also has a tendency to attempt to play God and to pass improper judgment on others. Unfortunately, it seems to be human nature to look for the failings in others in an attempt to feel better about ourselves. But when we speak evil against a person, it says a lot more about our character than about the object of our gossip (see Matthew 12:37).

Instead of using our words to judge others, it is time we used them to build others up. "Let everything you say be good and helpful, so that your words will be an encouragement to those who hear them" (Ephesians 4:29). The power of words is often underestimated by women. Just as words can cut down and destroy, they can also lift up and enlighten. When I feel a need to gossip, I try to change the subject from someone who isn't there to someone who is. And when I do, I try to find things that are redeeming in their lives or things that will encourage them. It isn't always easy to avoid gossip, and the habit of gossip is at times completely intoxicating, but as you turn it off, you not only draw closer to God through obedience to his Word but also keep yourself from drowning your mystery.

Another habit of the lips that is sure to bring death to any hope of romance is complaining. I confess that I'm a natural-born complainer, plain and simple, and I'm high maintenance by upbringing. I find great delight in discussing how much something bothers me or doesn't suit my desires. I feel compelled to complain about the weather, the food, the lack of service, or the general annoyance of being uncomfortable. When I think about it, I complain about almost everything, or at least I did. I hope I'm making some progress.

Complaining does two things to the man who hears it. First, it makes him feel like a failure. By his very nature, a man feels a deep burden to provide, and when a woman complains about something, he often takes it as a direct insult on his ability to meet her needs. Before I realized this fact about men, I was a slave of "total openness," meaning spilling all my opinions, whether or not they were better left unsaid. I can remember being on a date with my husband before we were married. He had taken me to a movie, a particularly bad one. Afterward he asked me how I liked it. I told him it was terrible and I could barely stand to watch it. I saw his countenance change, and of course I wanted to know why. I remember having to probe and probe, but he finally told me what a blow that can be to a man. He had planned a night for us, and I was unhappy with the evening. I had no idea that expressing my feelings in that way could be taken as a direct attack on his ability to provide for me. And though it was only a moment of conversation between us, for the first time I saw how my "openness" could hurt someone I loved.

Certainly I'm not advocating that we need to lie or tiptoe around to avoid hurting someone's feelings. But there's a way to express the truth gently, without complaining. Consider this: If you asked the man in your life how you looked in your new dress, how would you feel if, without missing a beat, he said, "Well, honey, you look fat. That's all there is to it." You'd feel awful, of course. Fat is never the right answer. So measure your words carefully—they can never be taken back. "Do everything without complaining and arguing, so that no one can criticize you" (Philippians 2:14-15). If I could do that movie night over again, I'd say to Michael, "Going to the worst movie in the world with you is better than going to all the Oscar winners combined without you! That said, not exactly *Gone with the Wind*."

Her Words Are Well Placed

Sometimes the temptation with our words is not how much we say but how we say it. When a woman tells a man what to do or pushes him to do something he's not stepping up to do, she communicates one thing to him: disappointment. And whether she is after his undying affection and lifetime devotion or simply his home improvement skills, when she asks in the wrong way, she doesn't end up getting what she wants. And romance suffers. As women we have an uncanny ability to communicate, but we are also able to throw those skills out the window when it comes to something that's important to us. Rather than picking the right moment and the right words and praying for God's help to bring about the change we desire, we forge through without any game plan other than "git 'er done" (man term). The trouble is that when there is another human being involved (especially one of the opposite sex), things are more complicated than that. And when a man is told to change this or do that, his first response is to push back.

That is why when a woman is dating a man she should allow him to define the relationship. When she becomes the initiator, the

mystery is gone. To be cherished by a man is to be pursued, even to the ends of the earth. And asking him to state his intentions leaves him no room to conquer, no chance for adventure. Why don't men stop and ask for directions when they are lost? Because that would thwart their masculine desire to work it out on their own, to find their own way. And so a smart woman knows that to step up and tell a man his next move, his next step, is to shred the veil of mystery that drew him to her in the first place.

For both the single woman and the married woman, words are the fertilizer that either enriches the soil of relationships or poisons the seeds planted there. Words define us today. And they are the legacy that will follow us tomorrow.

*Let everything you say be good and helpful,
so that your words will be an encouragement
to those who hear them.*

• EPHESIANS 4:29

Lifting the Veil

TAKE THE DAY OFF

Try taking an entire day off from talking. Mmm-hmmm, no talking for the whole day. I know for some it will seem like an impossibility. But see if you can do it. Tell your family and friends that you won't be talking for twenty-four hours, and then commit to it. After you start talking again, see if you notice a difference in the way you choose your words and the way you think about communication.

DROP THE G

Gossip can be a hard habit to drop, but in order to become a Woman of Mystery, you have to forbid it in your life. More easily said than done, I know. So take some time this week to figure out how best to let your friends know you've turned over a new leaf. Don't blame them or lead them to feel guilty. Make it all about your new experiment into the life of mystery. You might even want to make a list of things you can say when gossip starts to fly. Consider finding an accountability partner to keep you on track. And do what you can to wipe out the impulse to hear gossip by reading tabloids. Put some thought into getting rid of the gossip in your life.

her Style

Curve: the loveliest distance between two points.
• MAE WEST

Life is not the amount of breaths you take, it's the moments that take
your breath away.
• HITCH

The very fact that you are a woman means that you have the
uncanny ability to allure, delight, and fascinate a man. Your
femininity is a mystery to him. When he first encounters you,
he is intrigued by your lips, your eyes, your neck. He is charmed
by the lilt of your voice, the softness of your hands, the way your
clothes frame your body. Everything about you that isn't masculine
intrigues him.

But true femininity has little to do with natural physical beauty
or the clothes you wear and everything to do with the beauty that
inhabits your soul. Most certainly a man is drawn to what he sees,
but the truth is that what he sees is directly affected by how you

act and who you are. Take the case of an average-looking woman who isn't decked out in the latest trends but whose charisma captivates a room. She is interested in others and also interesting to them. Her style can make her the center of attention and draw the gazes of many a man, or it can express itself in the way she quietly captures individuals one at a time. People may be initially drawn to a beautiful, fashionable woman whose beauty goes no deeper, but she will never have that inner sense of style that a Woman of Mystery has.

If this style that captivates others doesn't stem from outward beauty or fashion, what is its source? It must come from deep within (see 1 Peter 3:4). And that is good news for all of us, because it means that the mystery that captivates men and sends them leaping from their chairs isn't the exclusive property of the beautiful, brand-name people.

The root of true style is the ability to live outside of oneself. People who meet you once and remember your name have style. When a woman compliments you with great thought and not just a quick "I love your dress," you notice. When someone is interested in you while all the rest ignore you, you are captured by that person's attention to you. Lady Diana was a good example of a woman with style. It wasn't just her physical beauty and impeccable taste—she had a mystery about her that captivated, a mystery that was founded in her love and concern for others. She was willing to live outside of herself, and she sought to help the sick and the underprivileged around the world. She once said, "Nothing gives me more happiness than to try to aid the most vulnerable of this society. Whoever is in distress who calls me, I will come running." Even after her death, she is remembered for her undying

her Style

desire to serve others, to be a voice to the weak and the needy—for her enduring style.

Her Style Is Modest

The style of a Woman of Mystery goes beyond her outward appearance, but it's also true that the way she presents herself is a reflection of what's inside of her. How a woman dresses tells the world a great deal about who she is and how she wants to be treated. A woman can beg and plead all day long not to be judged by her covering— her clothes—but what the world sees first, even before she speaks, is what she puts on in the morning. Clothes make the statement to anyone who is looking, "This is who I am; treat me accordingly."

When it comes to romance, clothes can play a significant role in the way a man sees you—and the way you see yourself. When you get ready for a romantic evening, you pick out what looks best on you and makes you look the thinnest and the most beautiful. But there is a fine line between wanting to look your best and wanting to look your sexiest. Everyone knows that a man is attracted to the female form. The curves that are unique to you as a female are enticing to the eyes of a man. But how can you decide how much mystery you should guard when you dress and how much you should give away?

On Christmas Eve, children fall asleep waiting for the time when they can open the beautifully wrapped presents under the tree. They argue about what is inside. They want to touch the boxes and shake them to determine if the contents will make them happy or simply keep their feet warm. A wrapped package brings much anticipation and hope for the one who knows it is for him. When a woman presents herself to the world, she tells people what to think about her by what she shows them. And men determine how to treat her largely based on how she presents herself. When a woman dresses like one of the guys, when she never gets out of her sweats and T-shirt, she is communicating a particular message about herself. And when she wears a form-fitting dress and high heels, she's saying something else about herself. So how can we find a style that fits us and makes us feel beautiful while still showing respect to men, to ourselves, and to the God who created us?

The first thing to remember when it comes to clothing is that men are visual creatures. That means they are turned on by what they see. On the surface that sounds like a good thing. After all, every woman wants to catch the eye of the man she loves. So why not use what you've got? The answer lies somewhere in the pages of that old leather book I told you about earlier. So let's open its pages once more and find some help on the subject of style and the men in your life. "You have heard the commandment that says, 'You must not commit adultery.' But I say, anyone who even looks at a woman with lust has already committed adultery with her in his heart" (Matthew 5:27-28).

According to Jesus, adultery is not simply a physical act, but it's a mental act as well. When a man looks at a woman who isn't his wife and lusts after her, he commits a sin. Not only that, but what an awful feeling to be gawked at and fantasized about by men you have no interest in whatsoever. And what about your soul? The men in the path of the sexy woman are responsible for dealing with the thoughts that she has induced, but what about the woman who left her mark on their eyes? Does she hold any accountability to God for her "revelation"? Before we get dressed in those low-cut tops or short shorts, we'd do well to consider the consequences of our choices. Besides the yucky feeling of being mentally touched by strange men, is there any reason to censor what we wear? The Bible has an answer for that. It goes against pretty much everything our culture tells us, though, so I pray that your heart is ready to hear it. "You must be careful so that your freedom does not cause others with a weaker conscience to stumble" (1 Corinthians 8:9). Matthew 18:6 says, "If you cause one of these little ones who trusts in me to fall into sin, it would be better for you to have a large millstone tied around your neck and be drowned in the depths of the sea." According to these verses, we are ultimately held responsible for the sin we knowingly lead others into. When a woman knows how her body affects a man and refuses to acknowledge her role in his temptation, she is running a very large risk to herself.

Exposing more of yourself than men can handle is not only a recipe for sin; it's also by definition mystery defeating. To the single woman who doesn't want to rush things, who wants to be loved

An Altering Experience

When your clothes are cute but too revealing, there are a few simple things you can do to make them work with your newfound convictions. I like something called clothing tape or body tape. It's really strong double-sided tape that you can get at lingerie stores. Use it to stick the front of your shirt to your body so that when you bend over nothing can be seen.

for more than her body, revealing parts of herself that a man finds sexually enticing is achieving the exact opposite effect. And for the married woman who wants to honor her husband and be faithful to him, choosing to reveal parts of herself to the world that should be reserved for him can leave him feeling jealous and suspicious. Certainly there are men who like to see their wives dressing sexy. They love her body and want to show it off to the world, but what those men aren't considering is the way that it compromises her and the men who see her as she walks down the street.

It is a tall order to change a sexy wardrobe into something more selective, and I know it. The first time I went to church, I wore a lacy black miniskirt, stockings and a garter belt, a vest, and not much else. I had no concept of lust as sin or my role in it. I was oblivious. So when a new church friend of mine finally brought my style of dress to my attention, I was shocked. And though I understood her words, incorporating them into my life was a struggle. I didn't truly understand the extent to which certain parts of my body, normally hidden but revealed by the raising of my arms or the bend of my waist, could affect the men who got a peek. And even now, after years of writing and speaking to girls about the trouble with choosing to dress sexy, I still have to occasionally ask my husband, "Can you see anything when I do this? And if so, what?" It's a bother, really. And it's not the easiest thing in the world to do either. Fashion doesn't much allow it. We want to be beautiful and alluring, so it's hard to resist a hint of cleavage. It seems so insignificant. But I know that's a woman's perspective, not a man's, and so I layer. I tape down. I lengthen. I do what I can to protect the eyes and minds of the men around me. I'm not a prude by any stretch of the imagination. I like being in fashion.

In fact, I consider being *ahead* of fashion a great coup. I was wearing dresses over my jeans ten years ago, before anyone else found it stylish. I want to set the trends, not follow them, so I don't need to be told that skin is in or less is more. I know what's cute, and I know how to make cute cover up the parts that need to be covered. So please don't think I'm asking you to put on your grandmother's housecoat or anything. All I'm asking is that you consider what it does to the men around you when you expose the sexy parts of your body to them. And then to do something about it. It's well worth it when you realize how much is at stake.

Her Style Is Frugal

Clothes carry with them an interesting source of both pain and pleasure. It can be a real source of stress for me to choose right, to find cute stuff, to dress well. All those things seem to forever plague this consumer's soul. Shopping can at times be a form of therapy and at other times be a source of anguish. For many of us, the mall is the place our hearts run free. As we see before us all the possibilities, we want to cry for pure joy. But what can also make us cry is our wallets. Clothes can be a strain on any budget. And they can also be a strain on a relationship with a man who really has no understanding of their emotional importance.

I once was a big proponent of shopping as therapy. When life was wearing me down, I felt a deep need to buy something. I'd go to the store and try something on, and I'd suddenly feel better— for a while anyway. Mission accomplished. But then as my credit card began to max out and my wallet began to starve, I had to make a few adjustments.

First of all, I had to teach my heart that clothes don't define me.

Sure, they explain me to the world to an extent. They give people a place to start understanding me, but they don't give me success or love. And when I bought into the idea that they did give me success, love, or even relief, I was assigning more value to them than they were due. In fact, I was giving them some of the role and worth in my eyes that should have gone to God.

Recognizing my tendency to go to the mall to find relief and the importance I gave to clothes, I chose one day to make a drastic change. Partly compelled by my idolatry of all things material and cute, and partly compelled by my out-of-control credit cards, I sought relief in the form of simplifying. Simplicity is consuming only what you need and nothing more. Simplicity is freeing because it takes the burden to satisfy you off material things and allows that job to be put back into its rightful place: the shoulders of God. "Satisfy us each morning with your unfailing love, so we may sing for joy to the end of our lives" (Psalm 90:14). So I decided to give away much of the stuff I had accumulated. I began by giving away ten things a day. Yes, ten things a day was my task. Give it away, sell it, or throw it out—the key was to simplify. And that's what I did. Of course the ten-a-day strategy didn't last for more than a few weeks, but it gave me a sense of focus that I needed to really reset my priorities. And it also did something funny to my shopping habits—it got me off the purchasing treadmill. It made me think twice before buying something that I knew I would probably just have to get rid of in a month. Whatever method works for you, I encourage you to do something to simplify your life and your purchasing habits.

The woman who is addicted to shopping, who collects shoes, purses, or jewelry, strikes fear into a man. He doesn't understand or

her Style

appreciate her fetishes, and he worries because ultimately he feels the burden of providing, even if she is bringing in half the income or more. When the credit card debt piles up, his temperature rises with it. A man can be intrigued by a woman who is thrifty and isn't quick to spend her money—or his! When a man sees that things aren't as important to her as people, he's attracted. And when a woman shows that she can meet her needs with concern for both finances and the environment, she offers a huge sense of relief to her man.

This hasn't always been the case, but right now shopping on the cheap is pretty easy in most cities. Rich people continue to give good clothes to secondhand shops. Discount stores get so desperate each week to clear out last season's stock that they cut prices to lower than what it would cost you to make the stuff yourself. There is a certain aura that surrounds a woman who finds value in making things work, who can get by with less and enjoy it. This woman can find pride in her ability to reclaim items that were previously loved and make them work for her again. She can consume less and give more. And the mystery that gives her a style so different from other women often compels a man to recognize and express his love for her and her wisdom in this area.

A woman who shops with the goal of buying only what she needs and living by the principles of frugality and simplicity gives the gift of mystery to her man and to herself. So let's make it our goal to let go of collecting stuff in closets on earth and choose instead to store up treasure in mansions in heaven. There is far more reward, both practically and spiritually, when we trim back on the stuff and major on what's really important.

Her Style Reaches Out

The world will tell you that style is all about *you*—a way to get what you want by turning heads and attracting people's attention. But for the Christian woman, style is not so much about what's on the outside (see 1 Peter 3:3-4). True style is about stepping beyond yourself. I am, by nature, a shy person in social situations where I don't know anyone. It hurts me—even makes me ill—to reach outside of myself and talk to strangers. I have an innate fear of rejection and disapproval. I prefer life at home, within my own four walls, with only those I know around me. But that isn't the life of faith God expects of me. When God called me to teach and speak, my quiet life changed. I could no longer hide in the comfort of my home but had to reach outside of myself to people around me who were looking for answers. That meant I had to deny my desire to look away from strangers and cross my arms, and instead I had to reach out and hug them. I had to learn to talk to people who intimidated me. I had to do things I was petrified of. For if I didn't, then I would be disobeying the very command of God to love my neighbor as myself. Most of my life I've longed for people to reach out and befriend me, to make an effort to get to know me and talk with me. But finally I realized that when I forced myself beyond my natural tendencies, I not only gained self-control but also learned to love as God calls us to love. And I was sold. Now, when I enter a room, I try to talk to the people there even if I don't know them. I found a secret that works for me. I just pretend that everyone already knows me and likes me. And I think to myself, *How rude would it be for me not to say hi?* I find that this helps me to get outside of myself and have compassion for the shyness of others.

A man is taken by a woman who can relate so well to those around her. Women are built for relationships, and when a man sees a woman who isn't afraid of that part of her, he is impressed. He is charmed by the woman who is fearless in her love of others, the woman who steps out and risks rejection to share the love of Christ with them. And I'm not talking specifically about sharing the gospel here, though that is an important part of our faith. What I'm talking about is loving people for who they are, the way Christ loves us. It's about caring for their needs, listening to their concerns, and making a difference, however small, in their lives.

If you're not sure how to begin reaching out to others, a simple smile is a good place to start. Kindness to strangers and even to acquaintances can be richly shown in something as small as a smile. When you look at someone, make eye contact, and smile, there is true style in that. Whether the person returns the smile or not, a gracious woman keeps the joy that is alive within her shining through her face. And people notice. It seems that everywhere you turn, people are looking away, refusing to make eye contact or sharing only a frown. It's hard to find the strength to reach out at those moments, but when you can muster the strength, not only are you developing an engaging style but you are also learning to walk as Jesus walked. His Word to us is clear: we must, as a matter of lifestyle, choose to love the unlovable, to care for those who don't care for us. Jesus put it this way: "If you love only those who love you, what reward is there for that? Even corrupt tax collectors do that much. If you are kind only to your friends, how are you different from anyone else? Even pagans do that. But you are to be perfect, even as your Father in heaven is perfect" (Matthew 5:46-48). God makes it clear that loving those around you, no matter how they may behave, is to be a part of your everyday life. And when God commands you to do something, he also helps you achieve it.

Her Style Embraces Life

A man is impressed with a woman who, regardless of her age, is in love with life. When you can drink from the cup, no matter how sweet or how bitter, no matter how empty or how full, and still find happiness and hope, your style is very attractive. Too many of us find something not to like about our lives, and when we do this, it becomes a heavy weight to the men who love us. The man in your life desires to provide for you, to care for you, and whether you are dating or married, when he sees you wanting what you don't have or longing for more of a life, he feels like a failure. Mystery is found in the life of a woman who against all odds finds joy. When a man sees a woman whose life is hard, who is up against daunting challenges, but who still loves life to the fullest, he knows he has found a good thing. Whether we pursue it or not, deep down all of us are wired to love life. Perhaps we've forgotten how, or maybe our to-do lists have squeezed out the time to enjoy what we do. But if we want to get back on track to find romance, we need to reclaim the love for life we once had, the full life God intended us to live (see John 10:10).

Consider the power of romance on your level of happiness. Who is sad when they are being romanced? Life is wonderful, and all is good. It's hard to get a person down who is in the midst of a wonderful romance. And maybe that's why we crave it so much. Romance acts like a drug—it numbs us to the problems around us and heightens our sense of hope and anticipation. I remember when Michael and I were dating, everywhere we went peopl would comment on our relationship. They talked about how happy we looked and wondered if we were newlyweds. Romance colored all that we felt and all that we saw in the world, and it was good. When I look back at that time, I see a better me. I see a me that welcomed the world, adversity and all. I see a me that was

9 signs you aren't exactly Ms. Charming

1. You talk louder than everyone else around you.
2. You use a toothpick after every meal, even in public.
3. You can out-burp most men . . . and you do.
4. You boss the server around.
5. You are picky, never satisfied, or you complain a lot.
6. You eat too fast or talk with your mouth full.
7. You talk about yourself more than you listen.
8. You find it hard to look people in the eyes.
9. You wear so much perfume that people walking four feet behind you can still smell you.

hopeful and peaceful, excited and energetic. I was all I longed to be, wrapped up in a blanket of mystery.

Now as I consider the true romance in my life—God and his undying love for me—I see an opportunity to live in the midst of romance all the time. Romance really describes the gifts of love from God, both those we covet and those we fear, like patience, perseverance, and trials. Everything that comes from God is meant to amplify the joy in life and make the pain more bearable. When I can look at everything that happens to me through the light of God's Word, I find myself deeply and passionately in love with life. And that love rubs off on everyone who is around me. Rather than being angry, crabby, frustrated, or burned out, I find myself delighted, hopeful, and confident that tomorrow will be better than today and that no matter what, life is a wonderful gift from an amazing God. To love life is to unlock the door to mystery and to find within the chance to let the truth of God shine through my every pore.

Her Style Is Honest

Unfortunately, one thing that isn't very easy for me is having a style that's true to me and my life, not a facade of what I want it to be. It's no wonder I fall into this trap, given the world and all its charms. With the tales of perfect love dancing before my eyes on TV and movie screens and the fantasy life I see in travel magazines and home journals, it's hard not to compare my life to this manufactured romance and start feeling empty. It's easy to say, "Why not me?" and "Where can I get me some?" when I look around and see that promised perfection just out of reach. My life never lives up to what I see in catalogs or on the screen. My days aren't carefree and effortless. My life is busy—too busy—and some days it feels like all I can do is get by and make it till the next day, when I get up and do the same thing all over again. I look at the lives of others and say, "When will my life begin? When will I get to live the dream?" And I start to buy into the lie that my life, this life I live day in and day out, isn't everything I need. I start to believe the lie that my style comes from something external, that my life matters or can give me joy only if it lines up with this fantasy version the world is selling.

It's so easy for me to lie to myself that I've had to create a moratorium on things like Pottery Barn catalogs. There was a time when looking at one would bring such remorse and hopelessness that it could send me into a tailspin for an entire evening. As I looked around my house and saw mismatched chairs and tattered table legs, I felt somehow incomplete. I looked at my married friends and I was forever hoping to be the bride myself. I wanted to get all the gifts and niceties I believed everyone else had. And so I grew discontented. But over time, and with much prayer and study, I started teaching myself a new reality. And that reality is that the things around me, and even the man next to me, don't define me. They don't determine my success or my joy or the way I see the world. Only God can give me what my soul craves, and that doesn't require anything more than a piece of ground to sit on and a light to read by. One of the great mysteries of life is how we can learn to be content no matter our surroundings. The apostle Paul was eager to tell others about his ability to "live on almost nothing or with everything." He explains, "I have learned the secret of living in every situation, whether it is with a full stomach or empty, with plenty or little. For I can do everything through Christ, who gives me strength" (Philippians 4:12-13).

Yes, it is easy to lose sight of the mystery that leads to true romance and instead opt for the manufactured romance promised by store displays and Hollywood. But the truth is that if romance is missing in your life, it isn't because you lack those things or those people you covet; it's because you have settled for an imitation. When we have finally had enough of the longing, when we realize that nothing manmade can define true style, then perhaps we are ready for more.

The style of the Woman of Mystery is the style of faith. Everything she wears and everything she does is colored by her belief that God's Word is the final word in her life. Your style speaks volumes about you—whether you are charming or standoffish, whether you love life or find it more of a bother. Your style is more than what's hanging in your closet. It's a reflection of your soul and who you are to everyone around you.

Lifting the Veil

SPRING CLEANING

No matter what the season, it might be time to do a little spring cleaning in your wardrobe. Set aside a few hours to pull everything out of your closet and try it on. Look in the mirror. Bend over, turn around, and try to see what others would see as you move. Could anything they see be considered a turn-on to the male libido? Find ways to fix that. Layer. Sew in a false camisole. Try double-sided clothing tape to hold your top in place. If it can't be fixed, get rid of it.

Taking the sexy out of your style doesn't mean taking the style with it. All you need is foundational clothes that can be built on by the addition of character pieces. Add a nice scarf to your T-shirt or bangles to your dress. Play up your individuality and express yourself with your own style. I'm here to say it can be done. If I could change my entire wardrobe and still keep my quirky style, so can you!

CENSOR YOURSELF

This week take an assessment of your discontentment level. If you find yourself discontented when you read your catalogs or magazines, ditch them. If you get depressed when you go to the mall and you can't afford everything you see, stay away from the mall. If there are certain shows or Internet sites that make you wish for what you don't have, come up with some other way to spend your time. Figure out what causes your emotional and spiritual grief, and find a way to avoid it from here on out.

her
Space

her Space

Remember, the shadows are just as important as the light.

• JANE EYRE

When you realize you want to spend the rest of your life with somebody, you want the rest of your life to start as soon as possible.

• WHEN HARRY MET SALLY

There is nothing as refreshing and comforting to a woman as her space. Her home, her room, her apartment, whatever the space might be, when it is hers it gives her a special feeling of peace and rest. Your space is your refuge. It is where you can rest from the battles of the world. It is a place to leave your mark, share your heart, and express your feelings. Some call it nesting, others call it making a home; whatever you call it, it seems to come naturally to most women.

I remember dating Michael when he lived in a big house near a lake in the middle of Washington State. He lived with a buddy of his in their bachelor pad. It was void of any feminine touches and notable only for its utilitarian purposes—a big-screen TV, large couches, a pool table, beds, desks, 4x4s, and a dog. That was all they needed. I remember going into the bathroom and thinking, *How do men live like this?* It was as if they didn't even look at the space around them. Of course, there are exceptions, but for the most part, making a space pleasant and attractive is a gift given to women.

For all of us, men and women alike, it can be hard to hear God in the crowds—hard to think, hard to study, hard to pray when the world is drowning out what's most important. But in the midst of your refuge, in the safety of your bedroom or resting on your couch, you can more easily sense God's voice breaking through to your heart. Many women who are married fail to consider that their homes are their husbands' sanctuaries as well. We can easily get caught up in our urge to nest and forget his need for his own space where he feels comfortable and manly. A woman who loves her man wants to create a space that considers him, his way of life, and his needs.

Her Space Has Room for Him

For a woman it can often be a difficult task to create a space where a man feels welcome or even included. We have feminine tastes, and we like to express them. But often those feminine tastes can come across as unwelcoming to men. We fall in love with flowers, overstuffed pillows, and incense, and we leave little room for dartboards, antlers, or big-screen TVs. And in doing so, we selfishly put our needs above theirs.

When we cover our homes from head to toe in shabby-chic softness or romantic French country, it doesn't allow much space for a masculine heart to breathe. But a man is intrigued when he finds a woman who is willing to include his masculine tastes and sensibilities into her design and nesting strategies. When a woman decorates with attention to a man's sense of beauty and utility, he is drawn to her. It shows him she is thinking not just about herself in creating her space but also about him. Certainly the way you arrange the care and design of your home is your and your husband's choice (or just yours, if you aren't married), but if you find that romance is lacking, it might not hurt to box up your inventory of dried flowers or Precious Moments figurines. In doing so, you are saying to your husband, "I am willing to love you the way you want to be loved and offer up unimportant things like collectibles in the name of creating a space conducive to romance for both of us."

This might sound foreign to many women, but it's something men are often hesitant or even fearful about articulating. Many men come home to a space that should be their comfort, their refuge, but instead it is filled with unchecked femininity and leaves them little space to relax and get the refreshment they need. Romance isn't dependent on setting, but romance can most certainly be scared off by its surroundings. So if you look at the space you've created and see that it has no room for a man's sensibilities, then maybe it's time to make some changes. Consider the man you love—or hope one day to love—and what might make him feel more at home in your space.

As a single woman, I knew that the home purchases I made would probably be the furnishings my future husband would live with, at least initially. So I kept a man's taste in mind in almost everything I purchased. I don't like to waste anything, so I didn't

her Space

want to buy super-cute stuff today and have to throw it out or give it away in a year if I found Mr. Perfect. So think about a man as you decorate. Consider making your home comfortable and inviting to his sensibilities. Buy less floral and more solids. Think about creating room for romance and masculinity, and you will be wisely preparing for your future.

Creating romance in a space doesn't require expensive furnishings or brand-name fashions. All it requires is some attention to the details that generate warmth and comfort. Lighting is key to a space. When I was just starting out on my own, I bought a cute little bungalow built in the '40s, and I set out to make it my refuge. Not having much money, I had to get creative. I found that the first and most important thing to attend to was the lighting. Harsh overhead lighting doesn't invite romance. But some inexpensive lamps to light the room add a degree of warmth and make an otherwise cold space cozy and attractive. Many women successfully decorate their space using preloved pieces of furniture. It's part of that growing trend toward simplicity, and it's another element that captivates a man. When he sees a woman choosing to live simply rather than extravagantly, it gives a man hope—hope that he *can* provide for her, hope that she doesn't just want him for his money, hope that she will be a satisfied wife and not one who continually covets what she doesn't have. Before I make a purchase, I always try to ask myself, *Do I need this or do I want this?* When my husband and I buy furniture for our cabin-style home, we consider two things: does it go with our outdoorsy style, and is it functional? In other words, can our daughter get food on it without it ruining our night? Simplicity ensures that things never take importance over people.

Her Space Is for Sharing

One of the most beautiful things a woman can do with her space is to share it with a heart of hospitality. God makes it a call on our lives to "always be eager to practice hospitality" (Romans 12:13). Hospitality, by its very nature, is alluring. It says to those who are offered it that they are important. And that provides an opportunity for heart change in people. There is a certain romance in the thought of a home filled with friends and family, love and laughter, a big table overflowing with food and people. Romantic movies like *Under the Tuscan Sun* and catalogs like Pottery Barn and Restoration Hardware all play off of this notion that hospitality represents the romance of abundant living. The more people who enjoy your presence and your space, the more joy there seems to be both in your home and in your heart.

Though I admit that it happens too infrequently in my life, I adore the concept of entertaining. I want my home to be a place of refreshment and happiness. I have romantic images of parties each weekend where we all sit around the table and share stories, hopes, and dreams. I imagine it, but I seldom pull it off. Lately, though, I have been making steps in that direction. The more I understand about hospitality, the more it compels me. I recently found an interesting dynamic about hospitality that I hadn't considered before. The *Tyndale Bible Dictionary* defines hospitality as "benevolence done to those outside one's normal circle of friends." And God's Word confirms it: "Don't forget to show hospitality to strangers, for some who have done this have entertained angels without realizing it!" (Hebrews 13:2). I had always thought inviting people into my home was mainly about friends and family. It is that—but also so much more.

The most significant obstacle to expressing this kind of unabashed hospitality is too big to ignore: the mess. It's so hard to get the house to a point where it is presentable. It takes a day's work just to get it where most of us can feel comfortable having guests. Statistics say that 98 percent of us feel good about ourselves when our houses are clean. And so when our houses are a mess, we certainly don't want to have people over.

I was once invited to a woman's home for dinner. It was a sweet little place, sparsely decorated. It didn't have any designer furniture or fancy curtains. The plates didn't match, and there were toys piled up in the middle of the living room. At first I was struck by the mess, but when she gave no apologies or disclaimers for her home, I quickly felt comfortable and welcomed. As we ate together, I listened to her and watched her face. She was happy and inviting. She didn't seem flustered, and she wasn't embarrassed to have me see her life in all its glory. In fact, after dinner, she actually gave me a tour of the place as if it were a magnificent mansion. She was genuinely happy with her space and wanted to share it with me, an almost total stranger. Days after meeting with her, I remember feeling more comfortable in my own space. As the toys piled up or the counters got crowded with our daily snacks and drinks, I felt less stressed about the state of my own home.

While I'm not suggesting that we let the mess of our lives remain a permanent condition or get out of control, I am suggesting that our mess isn't as much of a problem to others as we may think it is. Sure, if there isn't any place for people to sit and the dishes are starting to grow things on them other than what was originally served, it might be time to take action. A neat space is truly a refreshing space. It gives you room to move and room to breathe.

But if your space says, "I'm living, not obsessing," is that so bad? If things aren't as neat as they could be, you don't need to apologize. In fact, the mystery is when you are comfortable in your home and life and you allow others to be comfortable with you. Your life, in its unedited form, can be a great gift to others. So don't let the fear of judgment cloud your love for people and the truth that your space is a gift from God to be shared with others. Out of that you will find moments of great relief and great romance.

Her Space Is for Living

If you have a husband and family in your home, hospitality is not only for entertaining guests but also for providing for those who live in your space with you. The home is a refuge for you and your family, and because of that, offering a comfortable and peaceful environment for them is an act of love. Many of us are plagued by feelings of guilt and inadequacy when we consider how much we miss the mark in the clean house department, but I want to take this opportunity to give you some relief. Living and loving are more about being than doing. I know the dishes need to be done and laundry needs to be attended to, but you will never get today back. No matter if you're single or married, you will never get this time back. If you have children, then you will never see them at this exact age and this exact stage of life ever again. It will always be a memory, and now is when you can choose to make it a fond memory or just a blur.

No one knows what tomorrow will bring. And so sometimes we have to give ourselves permission to put the doing on hold and focus on the being. Practically that means that after your family has eaten and they are asking you to join them in a game of Candy

Land or Wii Sports, or when your friends call you up at the end of a long workday, you have to prioritize. What is more important at this moment in time? Cleaning up or offering yourself to the ones who love you and need you the most? Making some last-minute tweaks on that proposal or taking a break and getting together with your friends?

Since I had my daughter, my motto has been that living is more important than cleaning. It can be shocking when I say that to a group of women. They look at me as if I've just confessed the most unimaginable sin. But I'm not suggesting that we let the mess pile endlessly, just that we don't make the cleaning of the mess more important than time with people. For me, I have chosen to make evening time family time. After dinner we rinse the dishes and stack them in the sink, and then we play. We talk, we laugh, we wrestle, we unwind, and we enjoy each other's company. No matter your situation, I encourage you to find a way to say to the people in your life that they are always more important than things. When you can choose life over duty, you are living in a mystery that makes fertile ground for romance.

How well you pull this off has a lot to do with how you arrange your life. If you want to make the love of family your number-two priority after loving God, then you give yourself permission to do things differently. And what freedom and relief that brings.

Her Space Is Freeing

If we want our spaces to be places where we can relax and recharge and experience the grace of God—and where others can too—we need to make sure the feeling there is one of peace, not chaos. And for some of us, that means we need to release our grip on our stuff. Hoarding things as if you fear parting with them can be the symptom of a spiritual illness. And no woman should have to be a victim of it any longer. The key to setting yourself free from being a pack rat is to identify the objects that control you. The rule is this: anything you cannot part with controls you. And we cannot serve two masters (see Matthew 6:24). As Christians we choose what or who we serve: things, which are made by humans, or God, who made humans (see Exodus 20:4-6).

Some hoarders would argue that this is not the case—they are being frugal, saving things for a rainy day. And there is some merit in that, but we need to find a balance. When the thought of getting rid of those things that have been saved brings a feeling of anxiety and stress, frugality has lost out to fear. What an uncomfortable feeling to live with, even subconsciously, that we have to collect large amounts of things in order to keep ourselves and our families safe. Where is the hand and protection of God in that? God's Word tells us that we are called to store up for ourselves treasures in heaven instead of here on earth (see Matthew 6:19). An item hoarded is an item idolized. Those idols—items you cannot part with and that become more important to you than God—control you. If you can't throw it away, give it away, or sell it, then you've found your master. And once you understand that hoarding physical objects clutters not just your space but also your soul, you will find freedom. Hoarding puts God one rung down on the priority ladder, and it devalues those around us as well. The family and friends of a hoarder can feel overwhelmed and underloved because of the clutter that surrounds them and consumes so much of the hoarder's attention. We can't call ourselves followers of Christ and pack rats at the same time (although we can be recovering pack rats). If we allow our things to compete with Christ in our lives, we are making idols of them.

For the Woman of Mystery, balance has to be the key, and her desire must be to serve those she loves rather than to impress them or comfort herself. In her home, the Woman of Mystery finds peace and offers it to everyone who comes through her door. She doesn't allow herself to become a slave to any extreme: the perfection of her home, the neglect of it, or the collection of the things in it. This balance brings freedom to her heart. She is set free from the chains of her space and instead can enjoy it. She is liberated to open it to others and stop worrying about whether she will be judged. When a woman designs a space that not only creates a refuge for her friends and family but also invites God into it, she sets the stage for a life filled with true romance.

Lifting the Veil

DECLUTTER

Most of us have too much stuff, while others around the world (and sometimes in our own areas) don't have enough. When you declutter, you free up your life and can at the same time make someone else's life better. So make it your goal this week to give away, sell, or throw out at least ten things. If you like the feeling of liberation, make it your habit to do this weekly.

LOOK FOR NEED

Look around you, listen, and talk to find out the needs of those in your church, at your workplace, or in your neighborhood, and then see if you can meet them. In the family of Christ, there should be no one in need and no need ignored. If you can't do something yourself to help, recruit someone who can. Look out especially for widows and orphans (that might also include single mothers and children in one-parent homes). Give them food, care, company, practical assistance, or whatever they need. Just look for the need and then find a way to help. Develop your hospitality muscle.

HAVE A PARTY

There is no better day than today to start practicing hospitality. So no matter the state of your home, swallow hard and gather your courage long enough to invite someone over for food and friendship. When guests arrive, don't apologize for your space. Give them a tangible expression of God's grace by opening your home to them. Then put your calendar to work. Make it your goal to fill up one night a week or one night a month with friends, strangers, or whoever God puts on your heart to spend some quality time with.

her Waiting

her Waiting

I think I'd miss you even if we'd never met.
• THE WEDDING DATE

When ours are interrupted, his are not. His plans are proceeding exactly as scheduled, moving us *always* (including those minutes or hours or years which seem most useless or wasted or unendurable) "toward the goal of true maturity" (Romans 12:2).
• ELISABETH ELLIOT

A ny woman who has ever had a glimpse of romance in its purest form knows that it is good, and she knows she wants more of it. Whether you've seen it in movies or observed it in the lives of other people or experienced it firsthand, it only takes a taste of romance to want a full meal of it. Once romance comes into your consciousness, it continues to remind you how important it is to love's very existence. The imitation of romance can seem like a good substitute, something to stave off the grief of its absence, if only for a moment. But imitation or manufactured romance soon leaves us feeling cheated and lonely.

I can remember being single and going to as many romantic

comedies as possible. I wanted—no, needed—the experience of romance, even if it was only a vicarious one. But as the credits rolled, reality would creep back in and I would remember that I was going home not to Matthew McConaughey but to two cats and a tub of ice cream. And my heart was deflated until I got to the freezer. Of course, that's when other things got inflated! It was as if watching romance from a distance only made my lack of it sting all the more. And as I danced alone in my living room to Harry Connick Jr., I realized yet again how unfulfilling romance was without someone to share it with me.

He may delay because it would not be safe to give us at once what we ask: we are not ready for it. To give ere we could truly receive, would be to destroy the very heart and hope of prayer, to cease to be our Father. The delay itself may work to bring us nearer to our help, to increase the desire, perfect the prayer, and ripen the receptive condition.

– George MacDonald

Her Waiting Is Real

Waiting for love and romance to come along can be an emotionally exhausting experience. And when we seek out counterfeit kinds of romance to try to make the waiting more bearable, we only make things worse. Because after romantic movies, books, and music give us that taste of love, they quickly come to an end and leave us with nothing but memories of someone else's life, which is obviously a lot more romantic than ours. But in a way, couldn't we easily refer to all those romantic offerings as just emotional porn? Those counterfeits offer us a glimpse of the perfect romantic relationship, promising us that it exists just beyond our reach and then leaving us deflated and lost after we search for it in vain in our own lives. And like hard-core porn, doesn't emotional porn give us some kind of false belief that all men are divine, attentive, sensitive, and well built? Could it be that for the single woman these imitations only make matters worse?

Romance is such a powerful experience in a woman's life that we might need to consider how easily it could be used for our destruction. Most men have a pretty good idea that women crave romance, and I'm guessing there are a few scoundrels out there who use romance just to get something a little less than honorable out of a relationship. Love and romance can often be used to hold the heart of a woman hostage. "If you loved me you would." "I love you so much I have to have all of you." "Roses, dinner, a show? You owe me." Certainly romance can be used for evil, and that's why as women we need to be cautious, or at least as cautious as possible, when dealing with romance from someone who isn't our husband.

Only time can prove the genuineness of a man's affection. If he is angry that romance doesn't get him farther physically, then you can be certain his romance is not an expression of love but of manipulation. But the opposite can be true as well. We need to be wary of falling in love with a man who shows no sign of romance toward us at all. It's true that some men simply show their love in other ways than romance, but other times a lack of romance is an indication that he may not be interested in you in that way. If you don't heed that warning, or at least consider the yellow flag, you risk buying the lie that if you love him enough, one day he will love you in return. And that most often isn't the case. Men don't tend to get more romantic after they marry.

Many women live constantly in waiting, hoping that their friendships with men will lead to love over time. But in "just friends" cases like this, the woman is just a stand-in, a placeholder in the man's life. He sees her as someone to spend time with and have fun with but who he has no intention of loving or committing to. He uses her affection to occupy himself until true romantic love comes along. Romance is not always a sign of true love, and the absence of it is not always a sign of lovelessness, but in both cases careful attention should be paid to the state of the man's heart—and whether it's love he's offering or not.

Her Waiting Is Discerning

I once heard a woman who was in her fifties and had been single all her life offer this advice about marriage: "Don't be too picky." It's a phrase that is at once both completely true and completely false. While it's true that being too picky can leave you alone and lonely at the age of fifty, it's also true that women who aren't picky when it comes to love often settle for less than the best God could give them. So it's important to be wise in the assessment of who you are and the kind of relationship you deserve, and not to be so picky that you demand perfection when you yourself have no perfection to offer in return.

It can be said that one of the side effects of our hankering for romantic entertainment is that we set the bar for men way too high—as in nonhuman high. Romantic movies and books have a tendency to spoil us with an illusion of perfection. They don't show any brokenness or weaknesses in their leading men. They give us an unrealistic ideal to tantalize our senses. So when it comes to our own relationships, our minds can subconsciously determine that the man across the table from us should be the stuff movies are made of. And in turn, we are easily disappointed when we find no man on earth who comes close to our fantasies. But the truth is, it isn't a perfect man that God wants to give us. His desire isn't to give us what we want but what we need. And if he sees a need for a man who doesn't match your list, then your list needs to be ditched. Marriage is one of the biggest tools of sanctification in God's toolbox. In marriage you come face-to-face with a human mirror—someone who sees you with all your faults and all your idiosyncrasies, and who opens your eyes to them too. "It is God's will that you should be sanctified" (1 Thessalonians 4:3, NIV). Sanctification—that process of continuing to work out your salvation (see Philippians 2:12, NIV)—can be a painful experience. But "because we have these promises, dear friends, let us cleanse ourselves from everything that can defile our body or spirit. And let us work toward complete holiness because we fear God" (2 Corinthians 7:1).

Sanctification is required by God, and it also brings you a step closer to the heart of Christ (see 2 Corinthians 3:18). In your relationships (with men or women), if you refuse anyone who makes you think, anyone who challenges your status quo, anyone who questions your motives and calls you to a higher standard, you run the risk of walking away from a God-ordained vehicle for your sanctification. I often quote Hannah Whitall Smith because her writings are so rich in truth, and this one is no exception. "Look upon your chastening as God's chariots sent to carry your soul into the high places of spiritual achievement." All this to say: being too picky and demanding someone you never fight with, someone who brings you pure joy and never pushes you out of your comfort zone, may be tragic for your love life *and* your spiritual life.

However, you also can't just settle for the next man who smiles at you. That would be unwise. And such a state of mind only betrays a lack of mystery and an urgency to find someone at all costs. The more you believe in the power of God to put you with the man you should be with and the more you trust that getting the right man interested in you isn't a matter of your physical and mental strength but of your ability to withhold just enough to attract him, the closer you will get to finding the love of your life.

Romance between a woman and a man is a beautiful thing. When it is allowed to unfold naturally and is appreciated for what it is—an expression of one man's feelings for a woman—it is good for her soul. But when we place it on a pedestal, when we demand it as part of our lives, we run the risk of making it into an idol. When earthly romance is our elixir—that thing we are sure will cure all—then we've given it the role that God designed only for himself. Romance is not promised to any man or woman. It's not a requirement for love. So if you are married and you aren't finding the romance anymore, it's not because you married the wrong man. Regardless of why you got married in the first place, God promises to work "all things" together for the good of those who love him (see Romans 8:28, NIV). And when God says "all things," that includes your marriage. So your relationship, with or without romance, is not beyond the bounds of his plan. And your job now is to learn how to love God through it and to obey him in the midst of it.

It is my hope that each woman reading this book will experience the pure joy of being adored by a man. But even if that never happens, I can assure you of this: you are adored by someone more important than any man, and he is forever near and offering you a true romance that can never fade. It's only a matter of seeing him for who he truly is, putting out your hands, and accepting his love. In God's love letter you will find more affection and devotion than any man could ever give you. In it you will find complete acceptance and a steadfast belief that you can be all that you hope to be, plus more. God is on your side. He wants only the very best for you. And when you look to him, that is what you will get. Earthly romance is only a dim reflection of that which God offers to the hearts of those who love him. And one day it will be yours, twenty-four hours a day, for eternity. Nothing is better than that.

In the meantime, if you feel a romance deficiency, look for the romantic gestures of God. Spend time in his creation considering his handiwork. When you worship him, adore him, and get your mind set on the fullness of God, you will find more romance than you can handle. When you do, your craving for earthly romance will be greatly relieved. Being filled up on the true romance God offers will help you to be more discerning about the earthly romance you encounter.

Her Waiting Is Intentional

In the meantime, for my sisters in waiting, consider how you will live your life without the romance of a man. Will you wait passively? Will you get busy? What will you do while you wait? Before I got married, I used to say, "I'm not one to think that someday the UPS guy is going to knock on my door and carry me off in his

arms to a life of wedded bliss." I realized that being single required
two things of me: preparation and availability. I wanted to be prepared for a life with a man. And that meant that I had to have a
life—I couldn't wait for him to come and give it to me. What a
heavy responsibility for a man, and how clingy and unmysterious
of us if we need a man in order to have a life!

Early on in my single life, I began to prepare for a man, and
wouldn't you know it took me fifteen years of preparation to
finally be ready. But I am glad that those years weren't wasted—
they inspired not only my spiritual growth but also my emotional
growth. I took advantage of my single years as a time to get out of
debt, and later to travel and make the most of my singleness so I
would never resent not having lived enough or seen enough. I took
those years on my own as a time to improve myself so that I would
be a strength giver in a man's life instead of an energy stealer. There
were times I was sure marriage would never happen, but I didn't
give up. I ramped up my career, I worked on my house, I built a
life. I even, at one point, decided that one day I would like to work
from home so I could raise my future children myself. So I did what
needed to be done to arrange a life where I could do my work from
home. Of course, that required a considerable leap of faith as I left
my job at a major publishing house to strike out on my own, but I
knew what I wanted, and I believed I knew how to get it. Preparation. I tried not to waste my single years but used them to make
me the woman I wanted to be.

If you are single and find that you are waiting for your life to
start, then it's time to get to work. Don't wait for a man to be your
life, to create your life. Learn to cook. Buy a house. Decorate it.
Find hobbies you enjoy. Get out of debt. Learn to balance your

checkbook. However you imagine the woman you want to be, prepare to be that woman. What will you have to offer the man who melts your heart? Will you want to work after you have kids? If not, how can you make it feasible to stay home? Explore who you want to be, and then start planning and making moves in that direction. There should be no standing still when you are single; there should only be preparation. Of course, don't tell the next guy you date that you are preparing to be a wife—just let him see your life and figure that out for himself.

When you are waiting for love to come your way, you have the opportunity to prepare yourself not only physically and mentally but also spiritually. Paul talks about how much easier it is to serve God when you're single than it is when you have the cares of a marriage to deal with (see 1 Corinthians 7:32-34). Your single years offer a world of spiritual opportunities, and what you do with that time will affect your future marriage. If you neglect your spiritual growth and instead obsess over finding love, you will end up squandering precious time that could have been invested into your spirit.

Before you can find a guy, you're going to have to get out there. Be available—go where the men are. Take a class. Join a club. Go to church and be friendly. Risk life, and life will be your reward. If you're just sitting at home waiting for the phone to ring, where's the mystery in that? You should be busy and have a full life that invites romance and love into its warm embrace.

When I was thirty-six years old and single, I thought, like many other people, that all the good ones were taken. I wasn't spending my days with hundreds of eligible men like I was when I was in school. Pickings were slim, and I wasn't getting any younger.

When I made the decision to put myself out there and become more available for love, I had a choice. I could take matters into my own hands and take charge, pursue guys, make plans, and order my dating world, or I could walk out in faith and trust God to do the rest. And that's what I did. I made myself available, and then I let nature run its course. In other words, I put myself out there to get noticed and then waited for the right man to notice me and make his move. And it worked.

If you have already married the love of your life, there are still times when you need to wait intentionally. Waiting doesn't stop just because we are no longer single. We still wait for our men to pursue us, wait for them to figure things out, wait for them to fix things. Sometimes it feels like we are continually waiting for the men in our lives. And it can be easy to consider waiting an inconvenience and a nuisance. But we have the opportunity to show much grace to other people when we wait patiently for them to do what we wish they would do. Patience, or long-suffering, is considered a fruit of the Spirit (see Galatians 5:22). And that means that by the strength of the Spirit who lives within us, we can suffer long and still be joyful. We can trust in God's timing even when it comes to the men we thought would make our lives just what we wanted life to be.

Reversing Impatience

Some women get tired of waiting for a man to take leadership in a relationship, so they take charge themselves—in dating and in marriage. But I can tell you from watching it happen and hearing about it that once a woman takes over and runs the relationship, she is hard pressed to give back the reins to the man. And that means he will never step up and lead. He will expect his wife to do it all. After all, she did it all when they were dating; why change things now? So be careful how you start the relationship, because that is how it will progress. If you want to be cared for by a man, if you want him to arrange the romantic moments, then create the opportunities for love, but let him do the work.

If you started your relationship in the pilot seat and you want a change, then know that it will take some time. He will have to see a need, feel a need, and then fill that need. If he's been used to your taking care of everything—planning, arranging, etc.—then at first he will be shocked when you no longer do that. So talk to him about your change of heart. Apologize for any ways you might have hurt or mistreated him, such as being bossy or controlling. Humbly let him know that you want to change the way you do life together. Offer to let him be more in control. And then give him opportunities to make decisions, to step up and take the lead. No man who is unaccustomed to leading will do it until he is sure you are okay with him doing so. So give him chances to be the leader you want him to be.

We tend to forget that happiness doesn't come as a result of getting something we don't have, but rather of recognizing and appreciating what we do have.

– Frederick Keonig

Waiting is meant to bring purification. It is useful for drawing out the pollutants and bringing clarity to our lives. And the best waiting you can do is to wait for your Savior. You can be sure he will come for you and his romance will not disappoint. When a woman lives in tender acceptance of the hand of God in her life, she personifies mystery.

It's often said that just when you aren't looking for love, you will find it. And I think what that really means is just when you don't look like you are looking for love, you will find it. Because being prepared and available are ways a wise woman invites love to find her. Waiting can feel like a never-ending treadmill. There may be tears and sleepless nights, but when you take your focus off of what you don't have and put it onto what you do have, the waiting will be a time for beautiful growth.

Lifting the Veil

DITCH THE PORN

Do you have a problem with emotional pornography? If the viewing of romantic movies makes you discontented and down, then get rid of it. Say no to the romance novels and the chick flicks you turn to whenever you want to escape. When that escape leaves you feeling worse at the end, then it's really no escape at all. If anything your mind ingests distracts you from the reality of true romance as it comes from the heart of the Father, then maybe it's time to find something that's better for your soul. So decide this week what's bad for you in this department, and give up the porn. Then replace it with something healthier, like nonromantic novels, family time, study, or recreation. Rest and do nothing—just be. Think about life. Order your world. Find something positive to replace the thing you want to get rid of.

GO ON A DATE . . .

. . . alone! Get out somewhere where there is nature—an ocean, a lake, a park, a tree, wherever you can see the evidence of God's love for you. Enjoy the presence of his creation, and take time to listen for his voice, which draws you into the mystery of life. Sing your favorite worship song, and determine to find the romance in living.

her Worship

Take love, multiply it by infinity, and take it to the depths of forever . . .
and you still have only a glimpse of how I feel for you.
• MEET JOE BLACK

If I could measure the beauty of her eyes, I was born to look into them
and know myself.
• SHAKESPEARE IN LOVE

If romance is an expression of the love people feel in their hearts
for another, then worship is the finest romance a heart can experience. Not earthly romance, but true romance of the heart, mind, and spirit. For there is no greater love we can feel than love for God himself. And that is because of the great and unfailing love that he has shown to us (see 1 John 4:19). When a woman is truly living in the love of God and desires to express that love back to him, she finds herself in the grip of true romance. This kind of romance can feel strikingly similar to earthly romance. It lifts your spirit. It sends goose bumps up your arms. It brings tears of joy to your eyes and words of adoration to your lips. Worship is every woman's chance

to experience a life of unparalleled romance. Any other kind of romance we experience will be only a shadow of this truer kind.

Perhaps that's why we crave romance of all kinds so much—it speaks to us of the Father's heart. It reminds us how it feels to be in the presence of one who loves us unconditionally. And for a moment we are home, where our souls long to be: beside the Father. When I close my eyes and imagine one day crawling up onto the lap of the Mighty One, looking into his eyes, feeling his touch, and hearing his voice, it's like I'm transported to another plane of reality—the plane of worship.

But unlike most occurrences of earthly romance, the true romance of worship draws me out of myself while at the same time putting me in touch with the very core of my being. It is at once an outward expression and an inward washing. Nothing else can truly compare to this kind of romance. Worship changes everything. Through the eyes of worship, even the most painful and ugly experiences can result in sweet moments of comfort and protection between the Father and his child.

Worship requires action; it requires a choice to look upward instead of inward when we face the trials of life. It isn't avoiding the physical world but embracing the spiritual world. And it gives meaning to life. As humans, we cannot help but worship; it is in our blueprints. So we must worship—either God or something else. Worship says, "I live to serve you. You are my God—the one who gives me everything good, everything I need. You are worthy of my worship. You are all powerful and all knowing, and you hold my future in your hands." When we worship, we give honor to the one who loves us, saves us, and gives us hope. And worship proves the value of the one we worship to the world around us.

her Worship

Our modern Christian culture has taken the word *worship* and assigned it almost entirely to the act of singing and praising God, primarily in a church setting. Worship is that—but it is also much more. Singing God's praises is only the beginning of worship. It is a time when we are able to express our adoration for him. He is the Bridegroom who wants us to love him, admire his qualities, thank him, appreciate him. We were, after all, made in his image, so it is no wonder that the very things we desire are reflections of what he desires. And it is in adoration—through things such as song, thought, meditation, study, giving, service, and prayer—that we reach out of this ordinary world and into the life of mystery. Ultimately, mystery is generated not out of sheer brute strength but out of a mind and heart set on worshiping the one and only true God.

Worship in Words

True worship is determining to give God his rightful place as ruler of our lives. That means forsaking all other gods, even the god of self, which is a cruel taskmaster that demands more and more in an attempt to please ourselves. True worship, though, is first and foremost for God's pleasure.

Adoration

Worship starts with adoration. One of the ways we can express words of adoration is through music. The words of love and awe that we sing pour honor on our God and in return help us recognize his love being poured back upon us. When you adore God for who he is, you pour back his truth on him. You name his strengths; you appreciate his value, his love, and his person. And you make it known—not only to him but to your spirit as well—how invaluable he is to your very life.

Confession

The worshiper chooses to live in complete trust of the person and Word of God. And because of that, each day she is faced with the truth of her shortcomings, her inability to be holy as he is holy. We consistently remember the missteps and the messed-up moments of life that come out of our weak and tired hearts. But rather than retreating into depression, we look at our lives with the eyes of the one who sees everything as it truly is. We take note of our mistakes and confess them as such. It is in confession that we admit that we are not God and that we are so sinful we shouldn't even be able to approach him (see Psalm 51:4). When we come before him and confess all our sins, we remind ourselves where we have walked away from him and walked away from worship. We tell God that we agree with him that we have gone our own ways. Through confession, the Lord draws us to his feet and cleanses us of our destructive patterns as he forgives us. When we worship God, we agree that his thoughts are absolute truth. So whatever he condemns in our lives we also condemn, recognizing that this is for the betterment of our very souls.

And so confession is an integral part of worship. Confession is simply an agreement with God that his way is the right way and your way was the wrong. It is an acknowledgment that you sinned against him and him alone and that you feel sorrow about it. When you can honestly say that you are sorry for hurting God by disobeying his Word, you can be sure that your confession has been heard and forgiveness is yours for the taking (see 1 John 1:9).

Prayer

A heart set on worshiping God cannot fail to pray. For it is through prayer that we voice the truth in our hearts: that we believe in and trust the one true God. Prayer brings us to the point of expressing our complete reliance on the one who can be depended on completely. In prayer we come face-to-face with the faithfulness of God, and we present ourselves as available vessels, waiting to hear from him. Even in times of great stress and strife, prayer can be a way for us to worship. A missionary named Margaret Hillis knew this perhaps more than anyone else.

In the winter of 1941, while serving Christ in China with her family, Margaret found herself saying good-bye to her ailing husband, who was being carried off in a rickshaw to the nearest Chinese hospital. His appendicitis was life threatening, and he had to make a long journey to a faraway city to get the medical attention he needed. So when Margaret learned that invading Japanese forces were nearing her village, she had to make a decision. She didn't think her one-year-old son and two-month-old daughter could survive as refugees, so she decided to stay in her home with her children. She chose to trust God and pray for the best. When she awoke the next morning, she went to her wall calendar and tore off the top page. The day's verse was Psalm 56:3: "When I am afraid, I will put my trust in you."

The rest of the town emptied as all the other residents fled to avoid the attacking armies. The next morning she woke up and looked at her little calendar again. This time it showed Psalm 9:10: "Those who know your name trust in you, for you, O LORD, do not abandon those who search for you."

The next morning when she woke up, she could hear gunfire

in the distance, and she started to worry about how she would feed her children. That day's verse was Genesis 50:21: "No, don't be afraid. I will continue to take care of you and your children." That day an old woman came by with a pail of steaming goat's milk, and another person came by with a basket of eggs.

That night the gunfire got louder, and Margaret prayed harder. The next morning when she awoke, the calendar's verse was Psalm 56:9: "My enemies will retreat when I call to you for help. This I know: God is on my side!" That night as the battle got closer, Margaret couldn't sleep. But as day broke things got quiet. Eventually she started hearing voices, and she peeked out her window. It was the villagers who had left many days before. They were coming home! Suddenly there was a knock on her door. The colonel came to tell her that for some reason the Japanese forces had withdrawn. No one knew why, but the danger had passed and they were all safe. Margaret looked over at the little calendar on the wall and knew that she had been reading the handwriting of God.

When a soul prays, a soul hears from God. But when we fail to pray, we fail to listen. When God seems absent or silent, that's when we need to trust the character of the God behind the prayer and continue in it regardless of our feelings, knowing for certain that when the time is right, we will hear God's voice. The Woman of Mystery chooses to be driven by prayer. She designs her day around it. She never allows the cares of life to eclipse her time of prayer. She doesn't squeeze it in between this event and that event when she can but tithes her time, giving God the best part of it. Finding time for prayer can feel like an impossibility, since the loudest voices in our lives tend to get the most attention, but

her Worship

a life without prayer is a life without worship. And the Woman of Mystery must worship. Her very life depends upon it, because without it she lets the cares and struggles of the world cloud her vision and worry her heart.

Worship in Thought

What do we think about the most? What do we harbor, dream about, or fantasize over? It is our thoughts that define us. The thoughts that we allow to linger in our minds are the seeds of our feelings and actions. We first think and then act. Thoughts move us through our days and keep us in a state of anxiety or a state of hope. The choice is ours.

In 1933, when Ruth Bell (later Graham) was thirteen years old, her mom and dad decided to send her to a boarding school. Ruth was horrified at the prospect of leaving her parents in China while she and her sister were moved to Pyongyang, North Korea. She prayed to God that she would die before she woke up and had to leave. But that prayer was not answered.

At school Ruth was forever homesick. Daytime was not so bad, but the nights were the worst. Each night she cried herself to sleep, thinking about her parents. This went on for weeks until she finally made herself physically sick. In the infirmary she read Psalm 27:10 (KJV): "When my father and my mother forsake me, then the LORD will take me up." But even that didn't ease the pain. Finally she went to her sister Rosa and asked her what to do. Her sister simply said, "Why not take some verse and put your name on it? See if that helps." Ruth read Isaiah 53:5 and did just that: "He was wounded for *Ruth's* transgressions, he was bruised for *Ruth's* iniquities: the chastisement of *Ruth's* peace was upon him;

and with his stripes *Ruth* is healed." At that point she smiled, and her little heart began to heal.

God's Word was meant for you. And applying it to your life is the beginning of healing and hope. As our thoughts pore over the thoughts of God, we are uplifted. God's priorities become our priorities, and his promises become our hope. To live a life of mystery, we must consider our thoughts. We will not fail to grow whatever it is we plant. If we plant truth and hope, we will yield more of the same. If we allow our minds to cultivate thoughts of fear, envy, bitterness, and greed, we will surely grow the same in our lives.

In his great work *As a Man Thinketh*, James Allen writes,

> A man's mind may be likened to a garden, which may be intelligently cultivated or allowed to run wild; but whether cultivated or neglected, it must, and will bring forth life. If no useful seeds are put into it, then an abundance of useless weed seeds will fall in, and will continue to produce their kind. . . . Good thoughts and actions can never produce bad results. Bad thoughts and actions can never produce good results. This is but saying that nothing can come from corn but corn, nothing from nettles but nettles.

Worship colors our thoughts. When you worship, you cannot think negative or mean thoughts, only godly and hopeful thoughts. To change who you are, change your thoughts, and to change your thoughts, use them for worship.

Negative thoughts—thoughts that squeeze out the awareness of God in our lives—bring a heaviness to our spirits. "Letting your sinful nature control your mind leads to death. But letting the Spirit control your mind leads to life and peace" (Romans 8:6). Negative thoughts may offer temporary relief or satisfaction, but when allowed to dig into the soil of our hearts and take root, they make our lives complicated and our hearts bitter. They demand much and speak in a loud voice, blocking our vision from all the good in our lives. These negative thoughts shout, "I deserve more. That's not fair! I need that. I can't go on. Life's too hard." These thoughts are inconsistent with a life of faith but can occupy even the most godly of minds. Paul found himself in the same situation: "I love God's law with all my heart. But there is another power within me that is at war with my mind. This power makes me a slave to the sin that is still within me." But he goes on to give hope to all of us who struggle to conform our minds and thoughts to what pleases God: "Thank God! The answer is in Jesus Christ our Lord" (Romans 7:22-23, 25).

We must at every instance resist thoughts that are inconsistent with God's Word. It is easy to let painful or anxious feelings become our focus, even in prayer. We agonize over them as we cry out to God for relief. But Jesus commands us to "take no thought for your life" (Matthew 6:25, kjv). When we firmly choose to believe that God is big enough to handle whatever we are facing, we can state our case and then hand the thoughts over to him entirely, leaving them in the care of the one who cares for everything. Then we will be able to say, "Your will be done" and mean it in the very center of our hearts. It is a step of unfaithfulness to take on the cares of tomorrow. When we do, we're saying that we don't trust God to look after the practical details of our lives. But through prayer, we can take his hand and ask him to help us

her Worship

through the maze of our difficulties. When we take the time to realign our minds and focus on the things we are grateful for, we begin to cultivate a mind of worship instead of worry.

If we desire to turn from negative thoughts to good ones, then the reading of God's Word will be the vehicle of our deliverance, for it is the beginning of thankfulness. We are commanded, "Fix your thoughts on what is true, and honorable, and right, and pure, and lovely, and admirable. Think about things that are excellent and worthy of praise. . . . Then the God of peace will be with you" (Philippians 4:8-9). If we look around, we will notice countless things that are true, honorable, pure, and lovely. We can admire God's work in creation: the trees that are gently waving in the breeze, the smell of fresh-cut grass, the giggle of a small child. There are so many things around us to be thankful for, the biggest of which is God's Word. As we pore over the words he gave us, we find answers to our most probing questions. We discover reasons to hope and persevere. His Word never fails to satisfy the heart that is hungry for truth.

The study of God's Word brings us into worship and guides our thought lives. It teaches us who God is and what to believe about him. Without opening God's Word and putting our names in it, we fail to see the promises laid out for us. Without it we begin to feel the mystery fade as our minds turn to other cares. The Woman of Mystery is jealous for studying Scripture. She knows that it is the foundation of her life and her source of purpose and peace. She isn't anxious when the answers don't come immediately but is content to search God's Word and his true romance, trusting that through it she will draw closer to him, no matter what answer he leads her to. The study of God's Word is a requirement for worship and the beginning of all hope.

Worship in Action

Worship doesn't stop when the music ceases or the words don't come; it must continue through the actions of our lives. In the words of Richard Foster, "As worship begins in holy expectancy, it ends in holy obedience. . . . Holy obedience saves worship from becoming an opiate, an escape from the pressing needs of modern life." The way we worship is not only in specific times of adoring and enjoying God but also in choosing to live all of life with him in mind. We don't worship just to experience relief but to obey God. Who or what we worship will determine what we do with our lives. The worship of material gain will lead us to obsess over our work and income at the expense of those we love. The worship of contentment can lead to gluttony as we seek things like food, possessions, and approval to bring comfort to our troubled hearts.

Each problem in our lives can be traced back to misguided worship. When we give anything or anyone other than God the throne in our lives, we will inevitably get our hearts broken. Perhaps one of the draws of the Woman of Mystery is that her worship isn't divided. She denies idols at every opportunity. When her heart complains, when her mind demands relief from the discipline of godliness or a little downtime from the hard work of obedience, she shakes it off and reminds herself that the practice of godliness isn't what drains her, but her impulse to worship the wrong thing. It is a lie of the enemy that anything other than God can bring us relief.

Worship Serves

Worship is more than our words and our thoughts. It grows when it is in action. The outward action of someone who loves God is service. It is our purpose. "We have been rescued from our enemies so we can serve God without fear, in holiness and righteousness for as long as we live" (Luke 1:74-75). When we serve others, it is a way of worshiping the God who commands us to serve one another in love (see Galatians 5:13). Therefore, there can be no worship without service.

Service is simply going outside of ourselves—our needs, wants, and desires—and doing for others, caring for them, giving to them, teaching them. Service can come in the form of raising children—spending our days teaching them, nurturing them, and meeting their needs. It can come in the form of caring for the elderly, the handicapped, or the lonely. It can show itself in the form of teaching, giving, leading, or helping wherever needed. But it must come first to our family, then to the family of God, then to the rest of the world (see 1 Timothy 5:8; Acts 4:32, 34-35; Galatians 6:10). The Woman of Mystery gives generously to everyone around her, even if it is only the gift of a smile, a kind word, a hug, or simply her ever-loving presence. She is always looking for opportunities to give of herself, letting go of her fear of rejection, her tendency toward shyness, her insecurities, and her own desires, so she might lighten the hearts and loads of those around her.

I once knew a woman who so personified the idea of service that even in the smallest things she brought light to the lives she encountered. When she was around a waitress or a store clerk, she would ask for the person's name and talk to that person as someone who mattered. I watched her give life to many worn-out and lonely people who found themselves changing in her presence. Their sour faces gradually turned to smiles; their hearts

her Worship

opened up to this woman who saw them as human beings with real needs and hopes. She brought dignity to everyone around her, and in doing so changed her part of the world one smile at a time. It might not seem like much, but to one person, it might be everything. To a girl who is isolated from a world that has taken her for granted, a stranger who takes note of her can mean the difference between life and death. To a man who has decided that there is no good left in the world, a word of encouragement or respect can give him hope.

Service is a lifestyle. It is a conscious choice to see others as more important than ourselves, even those who could never do a thing for us (see Philippians 2:3-5). When a woman lives out this truth, she is alluring, and her lifestyle of worship is contagious. The Woman of Mystery is always aware of the aching hearts of those around her who long for attention and connection. She is a woman who looks at the world through the eyes of love.

The Worship Story

The Woman of Mystery sees her life as part of an epic story. She isn't an isolated individual but part of a bigger picture. She sees her life in those terms, and she knows that everything that happens to her is all part of advancing the story. And it's a story that must be told. She may not know why some things happen to her, but she is assured of the ending of the story. She knows that each scene of her life serves only to advance the plot in order to accomplish God's will here on earth. Just like Joseph (see Genesis 37–45), she has a vision in mind—an idea that each experience, no matter how mundane or heart wrenching, was planned in advance to serve a greater purpose. When we live with this kind of outlook, we find purpose and adventure and plot twists even in the bitterest and most ordinary moments. And so we are able to worship God and love others, knowing that each event in our lives is part of a sacred romance designed by a majestic God.

Lifting the Veil

PUT YOURSELF IN THE BIBLE

Take the lead of Ruth Graham and make the Bible real to you. As you read the Bible this week, insert your own name into the passages. Remember that everything in God's Word was meant for you. It will change you and draw you into the mystery of Christ.

WRITE YOUR STORY

Everyone has a story. How long has it been since you've considered yours? Take some time to record the times in your life when God came through in difficult situations, even if you weren't aware that he was near until long afterward. Write the history of your relationship with the Creator, then thank him for loving you so well.

the End

the end *(of a Life without Mystery)*

True romance, the key to all other romance, can never be fully yours unless you embrace the gifts of God as well as the trials of faith and the truth of God's Word. Learning to live in the mystery of God's love will awaken you to the love and friendship that is already around you. It will color the way you think, talk, and act. And it will help you not only to accept love from others but to love the way God made you to love.

I pray that true romance will infiltrate your life and that you will know you are not alone in your desires and your fears. We all face the same trials, as it says in God's Word: "The temptations in your life are no different from what others experience. And God is faithful. He will not allow the temptation to be more than you can stand. When you are tempted, he will show you a way out so that you can endure" (1 Corinthians 10:13). Take courage in these words. You don't have to be perfect, but the pursuit of godliness will bring you further and further into the mystery. Like me, you can probably expect to take two steps forward and one step back. It's normal, and you can't let it deflate you. Life isn't all about forward movement. It ebbs and it flows. You are not abnormal in that fact. Just take heart in the fact that we are all in this together.

In the name of togetherness, I encourage you to keep the conversation about romance and mystery going, and to bring other women onto the same path toward true romance. To connect with others sharing this journey and for more books to read on this topic, log on to www.thewomanofmystery.com, where you can share your stories, both heart wrenching and heartwarming, and encourage others in your common pursuit of true romance. I'll be there too as we unveil these secrets together. I look forward to hearing from you!

HAYLEY DiMARCO is the best-selling author of more than thirty books, including *Dateable* and *Marriable*. She spent the early part of her career working for a little shoe company called Nike in Portland, Oregon. After three years with the "Swoosh," Hayley got fed up with the incessant rain of Portland and began to search for drier ground. Soon she found just the spot: Nashville, Tennessee, where she became the manager of promotions at Thomas Nelson Publishers. While operating as the brand manager of Nelson's new teen line, Hayley authored, edited, or had her hand in more than thirty-six different titles.

In 2002 Hayley left Nelson and founded Hungry Planet, a company intensely focused on feeding the world's appetite for truth by producing books and new media, taking on issues of faith and life with a distinctly modern voice.

Shortly after founding Hungry Planet, Hayley successfully completed a nationwide executive search for someone to run the company so she could focus on writing. She describes her husband, Michael, as her most successful business acquisition! Hayley and Michael are now the proud parents of Hungry Planet's thirty-plus books, including ten best sellers, three ECPA Christian Book Award finalists, and one ECPA winner, and one amazing human, their daughter, Addison.

Join Hayley and *The Woman of Mystery* conversation at thewomanofmystery.com.